THE IMPOSTER CURE

THE

YOU ARE NOT A FRAUD.

IMPOSTER

YOU DESERVE SUCCESS.

CURE

YOU CAN BELIEVE IN YOURSELF.

How to stop feeling like a fraud and escape the mind-trap of imposter syndrome

Dr Jessamy Hibberd

Dedicated to Jack

An Hachette UK Company
www.hachette.co.uk

First published in Great Britain in 2019 by Aster,
an imprint of Octopus Publishing Group Ltd
Carmelite House, 50 Victoria Embankment
London EC4Y 0DZ

Distributed in the US by
Hachette Book Group
1290 Avenue of the Americas
4th and 5th Floors
New York, NY 10104

Distributed in Canada by
Canadian Manda Group
664 Annette St.
Toronto, Ontario, Canada M6S 2C8

ISBN 978-1-78325-306-7

A CIP catalogue record for this book is available from the
British Library.

Printed and bound in the UK

1 3 5 7 9 10 8 6 4 2

Consultant Publisher: Kate Adams
Editor: Ella Parsons
Copy Editor: Mary-Jane Wilkins
Designer: Jack Storey
Typesetter: Jeremy Tilston
Production Manager: Caroline Alberti

You are not a fraud

When I excitedly told family and friends about this book, the most common response was, 'I think I've got that – is it normal?' Many times I saw a flash of recognition immediately followed by an expression of relief as they thought, 'I'm not the only one.'

Everyone had a story.

'My sister is brilliant at her job, but she's always telling me that she can't understand why her colleagues think she's any good.'

'I felt like that when I got accepted on to the doctorate course.'

'A guy at work was telling me the other day how he feels like he's just winging it – he's got three kids; he's so successful but he clearly thinks he's inches away from being sacked.'

Imposter syndrome isn't something that only *you* are suffering from. It's something we can all relate to. We all know that feeling, whether it's with you all the time or just in certain situations. It's the feeling you experience when you start a new job, when you get a promotion or when you are accepted on to a course. It simply means you care about what you're doing, that you want to do a good job, but that you're worried you're not up to it.

As I've researched this book and delved deeper into this world, I've come to realize that imposter syndrome involves much more than just feeling fraudulent and that it presents itself in a long list of different ways. It may appear as insecurity, self-doubt, fear of failure and perfectionism. Or as self-criticism, low self-esteem, an inability to accept compliments or a focus on where you're falling short. It's a guard against arrogance and a safety net in case everything goes wrong. This list, rather than being titled 'Imposter Syndrome', could be titled 'The Problems of Being Human'. This is a collective experience, which is why it is time to talk about it openly because it is holding so many people back from fully engaging in life.

Before I started writing this book this wasn't a conversation I'd had with my friends or family. Because of the fear and shame attached to imposter syndrome, there are rarely opportunities to talk about these feelings and discover that it's not just you who feels this way.

This book aims to open up the conversation about imposter syndrome. I hope it will help you and many others see that this feeling doesn't mean you're lacking in some way; it just means you're not sure if you can do what you set out to do yet. When you recognize that this feeling is not proof that you are an imposter but a normal discomfort that everyone experiences, you will be able to respond differently. With awareness and practice you will find it possible to develop a healthy relationship with fear, vulnerability and failure and this will prevent these emotions from limiting you any more. Not only that; you will be able to open up and take a fresh look at your life, thinking about what you want to be, now and in the future.

I hope you enjoy the book. And remember: you've got this, you are not a fraud, you deserve success and you can believe in yourself. It's time to escape the mind-trap of imposter syndrome!

Introduction: You are not alone

We might not know each other and I haven't had a chance to hear your story. But I'm pretty sure I already know a lot about you.

You've been carrying around a secret that's kept you living your life in a state of low-level fear, wondering when you'll be found out. You've fooled everyone into believing you're better than you are, putting on an act of knowing what you're doing and working extra hard to avoid detection. If people really *knew* you, they'd see the cracks in the surface. Most of your big accomplishments have just been luck or the result of being in the right place at the right time. In truth, you're an imposter.

You might not feel this way all the time, but when you do, this pervasive self-doubt and insecurity creates a cloud over everything you do, a constant nagging feeling of stress and anxiety, which affects both your work and your relationships. This might push you to keep reaching for perfection, but as perfection doesn't exist you rarely feel satisfied or content with your achievements or with who you are.

Family, friends and colleagues see you as capable and accomplished. They don't know about your inner turmoil. To them it seems that everything is OK or, better than that, they think you're doing well. They may even wish they were doing as well as you. But you *know* they've got it wrong. You're just putting on a front – you're good at giving the impression that you're competent. The version they see is far from the truth.

On the rare times you do open up to family or close friends, they dismiss your concerns, unable to match up what you're saying with what they see you as capable of. They may feel that you need to have your ego bolstered when in reality you are simply scared. As a result, you often feel misunderstood and that no one else knows the full extent of your feelings.

Only you know the truth; that you're just scraping by. You have to work harder than everyone else to prevent anyone discovering who you really are. Or you procrastinate terribly when given a big task and put together half your projects seconds before the deadline. You're nothing special and are only where you are thanks to luck, contacts or because you worked harder than everyone else. When you do well, which you almost always do, you tell yourself anyone could have done it. You were just in the right place at the right time. You might have managed it this time, but how long can it last? When things don't go according to plan, this is all you can think about; self-criticism weighs in as you repeatedly replay what went wrong in your mind.

If you've been given positive feedback you think that's just because people like you and they're being nice. It was the team's success more than yours. Whereas if you make a mistake, it's all yours. You have a library of responses up your sleeve and you're armed and ready to use them. So no matter what you do, you find it impossible to take on board your successes.

You hold tightly to the belief that you aren't good enough and you've been methodically building your argument to support this belief in your head for years. When you hear any scant evidence that fits with it, you're all ears, while anything that doesn't fit with this view is dismissed. No matter how much evidence there is to contradict your view, you're unable to internalize your accomplishments and you feel uncomfortable when praised. This makes it almost impossible to own your achievements or to see yourself as competent and able. Even if you've been in your job for years, this feeling stays with you as your view of yourself remains unchanged.

When you do well or things work out yet again, this doesn't help – it only makes it worse. The more success you achieve, the more pressure you feel as your responsibility and visibility increase. Instead of questioning yourself or changing your view, you just feel relief that you've managed to succeed this time and that no one has discovered the truth. You've got away with it again.

This feeling ruins the moments when you achieve your goals or simply do something great. You quickly sweep these away, sure that you're even more likely to be found out now. Even the best occasions are tainted by it. You rarely celebrate your achievements or feel comfortable and easy about doing well. It's so much harder to enjoy life when you're carrying this weight around with you.

Eve knew this all too well.

When they told Eve she'd got the job, she just felt shock. When she'd applied for it, there was no part of her that believed she'd actually get it. She clearly wasn't the same calibre as the other applicants. They were all graduates and she only had on-the-job experience. She'd got terrible grades at school and had been lucky to find a job she could stick at. She'd worked hard and had some good connections, but she was nothing special. If she could do this, anyone could.

People always warmed to Eve. She knew she made a good impression in interviews, but that was just superficial stuff. Anyone could fool people into believing they could do something when they'd only spent an hour with them. It was much harder to keep this belief going when you were part of a company and seeing these people every day. She was in way over her head.

The company may have overlooked her grades because they'd liked her so much, but would they still like her when they saw her work wasn't as good as everyone else's? She knew they'd made a huge mistake; she felt it deep in the pit of her stomach alongside a crippling self-doubt. The only way she was going to get through this was to keep attention away from herself. Get everything done, work hard at it, keep going and never make a mistake.

Eve felt terrified at the start of every new project, but she somehow managed to pull everything together every time there was a deadline. She worked long hours and at weekends to hide the fact that she was struggling. She took a painfully long time drafting emails to check the wording and accuracy, and was unable to share any of her work until it was perfect.

Meetings filled her with dread; she wanted to speak up, but she never risked it, in case she exposed herself. When she did have to present, she agonized for hours over her presentation, practising and practising until she knew it off by heart. She rarely took holidays, as her absence might give people a chance to see what was really going on and, despite encouragement from her manager, she avoided the bigger projects.

On the rare occasions she did get negative feedback, it crushed her, staying with her for weeks, as she went over and over what had been said. It didn't seem to matter how much positive feedback she got or how much she accomplished, she couldn't shake the feeling of failure.

She managed to keep things going, just, but every time she got over another hurdle she'd feel exhausted at the prospect of having to do it again. She thought she might grind to a halt under the weight of it all.

Everyone thought she was brilliant, but that just made everything worse. It was only a matter of time before they discovered the truth. Her success was undeserved; they should never have taken a chance on her in the first place.

When you're plagued by these fears you're in a very lonely place. You overwork, focusing only on your mistakes, and are fearful of speaking up or taking a wrong step. At times you avoid everything. While Eve's experiences may fit with some of your own, I'm sure you can also see that she isn't completely right about herself. How can she be doing this well, receiving positive feedback and seen as brilliant, if she really is no good at her job? Does liking someone really mean that people overlook everything else?

There's a name for how Eve is feeling: imposter syndrome. And the trouble with imposter syndrome is that it can make you reach conclusions that don't quite add up. You'll find what I'm going to say next harder to believe, but bear with me.

You are intelligent, you have already achieved things (otherwise what would you have to doubt?) and I'm guessing you have a proven track record of success. You have qualifications and a good job. You may even have several degrees. Imposters like to be well trained before they can acknowledge that they're experts!

Maybe you didn't go to university or college, but now you are doing really well, as Eve is. Yet, surrounded by graduates, you're not sure how you got there. Perhaps you're doing better than you expected, moving up the career ladder faster than you thought you might, especially in comparison to others you see as more intelligent or more likely to succeed than you. Maybe no one expected you to do well and you believed this too.

By most people's standards you are considered successful, but you don't see yourself this way. And that's where the problem lies. There's no issue with what you're doing by anyone else's standards. It's how you view yourself that is the problem.

As you'll see as you work through this book, how you define success is key. And success is different for everyone. It doesn't necessarily mean being the very best at everything you do. It doesn't need to mean a first-class degree, status, fame or fortune. But even if those things are important to you, if you are unable to internalize any of your successes your view of yourself can never change.

There's a small part of you that knows you're doing well; you see glimpses and occasionally feel it, but those moments don't last long. They're fleeting and hard to hold on to, often drowned out by the louder, more confident and far better rehearsed voice that tells you you're an imposter. This makes it difficult for you to create a different view of yourself that is more consistent with what others see.

Overcoming imposter syndrome

How do I know this about you when we haven't even met? I know because this is how imposter syndrome operates. It's a common feeling that, left unchecked, can have a corrosive impact on your life. I know because it doesn't just affect you. You're not the only one who feels a fraud. In fact, so many people do that psychologists came up with a name for it and a set of symptoms. I hope that knowing this brings relief. There's something about putting a name to something that takes away part of its power. Knowing what it is gives you options and makes it easier for you to identify it. Then you can find ways to change the belief – something we'll be doing in this book.

Imposter syndrome doesn't discriminate; it affects everyone from college students to CEOs. People from every demographic who are clever, driven, articulate, creative and successful have difficulty in acknowledging their achievements.

In my work as a clinical psychologist, I regularly meet people who experience imposter syndrome – they are interesting, hard-working and their list of achievements is always impressive. Everything they need to enjoy their life is within reach, but because of their feeling of being an imposter they just can't see this. Often the real problem is an underlying fear of not being good enough. It's my job to show them what I can see in them and help them connect to this new view, building their confidence and belief in themselves so they can enjoy life again.

To do this we identify together how imposter syndrome operates in their life, look back at what may have caused it and re-evaluate old beliefs. We build an argument against it and a new and more realistic view of what competence means. I've helped many people beat these feelings and I know I can help you too. I'll be sharing all the ideas and strategies I use in therapy with you, so you can move forward, find confidence and develop a new view of yourself.

I don't just see imposter syndrome in my clinic; I see it among my friends and family and I've experienced it myself. The first meeting I had about this book went well and I felt that the publisher and I had really connected. As soon as we walked out of the door, I turned to my brilliant agent Jane and said, 'You know I'll need a really good editor if I get this. I don't think my writing is up to it.'

I'm sure you can see imposter syndrome in Eve. You might have seen it in others too; in fact you can feel shocked when some people tell you their truth, but you can't always see it in yourself.

I'll be including case studies such as Eve's throughout the book. It can be easier to see how imposter syndrome operates when your own emotions aren't involved. The better you become at recognizing the syndrome in others, the more you'll be able to see it in yourself. Each case study is based on interviews with real people, but the names and some details have been changed for confidentiality.

I hope reading this will make you feel a little less alone. If there's a whole book on this and I see it again and again in my clinic, then you can't be the only one. When you see how common it is you may begin to notice – even if only for a moment – that there's something else going on here. And maybe, just maybe, you're not right about yourself. We can't all be imposters, can we?

You are not an imposter

I can confidently tell you that you are not an imposter, even though I've never met you and even though I don't know the specific details of your story. But I know that this isn't going to change your mind (yet). If it could, you wouldn't need this book.

I want you to know that there is nothing wrong with you. You have no reason to be ashamed. You've been suffering under a mistaken belief and this has stopped you from being able to speak up. It's time to get this fear out in the light, to question it and show it up for what it is – a faulty belief.

The fact that you've picked up or downloaded this book is a really good sign. You don't want to continue to live like this – feeling as though you're winging it, that you are moments from being found out and humiliated. You're ready for a change. But I also know that the solution is not as simple as just wanting to change. If it was that easy, you'd have let go of these feelings a long time ago.

So if you can't go with me yet think of this another way. Things aren't working for you at the moment. These thoughts are holding you hostage. They might tell you they're keeping you safe, but they're keeping you away from life and the enjoyment of all its pleasures.

Can you really continue to live your life like this, condemning yourself to feeling constantly on edge? Does this feeling sour every new promotion, job change or salary increase; does it filter into your relationships, leaving you unable to show your true self for fear of exposure?

You know from experience that further training or success will not change this. The only person who can change this is you.

If you fast-forward through your life and visualize a future in which you have never tried to change, won't there be some regret? Wouldn't it be better to look back and know you tried? Won't there be more relief and comfort in knowing you've done all you can? What have you got to lose? If you don't try, nothing can change – at least trying means giving yourself a chance at a different life. This might seem scary, but the potential reward is huge. Let me give you this chance.

Here's what we will do and how it will help you:

- You'll free up so much mental space as you'll no longer be dealing with all the problems that arise alongside imposter syndrome: the emotional drain, the heavy weight, the sheer capacity it takes up.

- Together we will build a dossier of evidence to show you that you are not an imposter. This will be based on facts rather than thoughts and feelings, so you can let go of the old beliefs and coping strategies that are holding you back.

- You will develop compassion for yourself – it's the perfect antidote to the self-critical and perfectionist thinking that can lead to stress, anxiety and depression. This will support you to make the changes you need to, so you no longer feel stuck.

- You'll see that it's OK to make mistakes and will learn to take failure in your stride. When you accept mistakes and failure as normal and see them as an opportunity to learn, grow and increase resilience, you will find it much easier to let them go.

- I will show you that insecurity and confidence are not separate but intertwined. Everyone experiences insecurity and lacks confidence at times and there is strength in vulnerability. You'll see that no one has it together all the time.

- You'll start to enjoy life again. Self-doubt, overwork and procrastination will become a distant memory. You will experience less anxiety, have closer relationships and face challenges head-on. This will help you to open up, take risks and have the confidence to try new things.

- More than that, you will have an opportunity to see what you're really capable of; a chance to give a voice to the small part of you that knows you could be great. There will be an opportunity to learn new things about yourself and the world; a chance to embrace life and go for it.

I know what you're thinking: 'But I really am an imposter!' Imagining a different reality might feel impossible right now. All I'm asking of you is to be open to change. It may not be easy but wanting to change makes a massive difference. Seeing that there's an alternative offers hope, motivation and the possibility of living differently.

I would like you to see yourself as others do, but ultimately it doesn't matter what I or others think. What matters is how you see yourself and it's this I'm determined to change, so you can trust yourself and see just how capable you are.

To do this, you're going to need to trust me and give me a chance to convince you. These ideas and techniques are based on my 14 years of clinical experience, my training and all the evidence-based research in this area. You may have had this idea about yourself for a long time, but that doesn't make it right. When you read this book hold the ideas in mind and try them on for size. Attempt the strategies and allow yourself to think differently. I promise you won't regret it.

How to get the most from this book

This book will increase your knowledge and understanding of imposter syndrome. It will help you see how it operates and why, so you can break old patterns and escape its clutches. It will teach you the skills to overcome it, increase your confidence, show you how to take risks and embrace mistakes and failure (I know you can't believe this yet). Most importantly, it will help you gain a more secure and accurate self-image, so you get to know yourself better, learn to accept positive feedback, have closer relationships and – finally – begin to believe in yourself.

The aim is to help you see yourself differently and gain new perspectives. Imagine you're on a mountain. Until now you've been standing halfway up, believing that you're seeing an accurate picture of life. I want to take you further up the mountain to a higher vantage point, where you'll have a far better view and can see the world as it really is.

For this to work, you'll need to do more than just read the book; you'll need to translate the ideas into your own life and try out all the strategies (yes – all of them). This is a bit like learning to drive: it's all very well passing your driving theory test, but that doesn't teach you how to drive a car. Psychology is the same. The theory is really helpful (and interesting) and a first step towards understanding your mind better, but putting these ideas into practice and carrying out the strategies will really make a difference to how you feel.

The myth of imposter syndrome

It makes me work hard

It keeps me humble

It means I aim for high standards

It motivates me

It is better to be modest than arrogant

It keeps me in check

Often people try to convince me that imposter syndrome has its good points and say that it's not all bad. They believe it brings some advantages, that their imposter feelings are a way of ensuring that they don't become arrogant. Also they think that if you underestimate yourself this will motivate you to improve – it makes you work harder, aim higher, do better. It keeps you on your toes, stops you getting big-headed or complacent and will protect you if everything goes wrong. You may feel that it's who you are, which makes you cling to this identity – it has got you this far, so it must be working; it feels risky to try another way.

So before we begin I want to make it clear that there are *no* advantages to holding on to imposter syndrome! Rather than helping you, imposter syndrome has been holding you back. It makes you feel more anxious, it stops you taking on board any of the good things you do and makes it difficult to enjoy the things you care about. In this book I will show you both the sacrifices it has forced you to make and the limits it has put on your potential achievements.

Of course, no one wants to be arrogant or lack insight, but overcoming imposter syndrome will not cause this. What you are doing is not being modest but putting yourself down. Acknowledging your own skills, knowledge and experience is not arrogance.

Imposter syndrome is *not* what pushes you or makes you good at what you do; you are the one that does this. You are hard-working and conscientious; that is the person you are. Wouldn't it be better to be ambitious, take on challenges, have humility and courage without the anxiety imposter feelings can bring and the cost to your health and happiness? Would you like to be able to enjoy your successes and go for the things you want, without these old fears holding you back? You'll soon have a chance to see how much better life is without it.

Three key steps to success

Step one: wanting to change
Step two: understanding the theory
Step three: trying out the strategies

Good logic won't be enough. You're going to need to follow all three steps for this to work. You need to want to change, to really listen to the new evidence and you have to test it out. Most importantly – and for some people this will be the most difficult part – you need to let go of the need to be right.

I know it's hard to stop and do the exercises, but please give them a go the way I'm suggesting. An idea is less persuasive than actual proof. And you're going to need proof. You've already been told many, many times that you're not an imposter and, so far, it has made zero difference.

Try *every* strategy, even the ones you think you won't like. In therapy, I find people are often surprised by which strategies work best for them. It's a bit like buying new clothes: as you browse you pick out the ones you like, but you can't know how they'll look and whether you like them until you try them on. It's only when you're wearing them that you can tell which suit you best.

And just as with clothes, there's no 'one size fits all' – you need to work out what suits you. Different approaches work for different people and by trying out all the strategies you'll find a range of options that work for you. The more you do, the better chance you will give yourself and the more arguments you'll store up against the imposter message.

It's also important to talk to others about it, to actively open up the conversation. You'll be (pleasantly) surprised how many people will relate to the way you feel. Start paying attention to it in day-to-day life and seek out others who experience it, whether it's someone well known or a friend, colleague, family member or acquaintance. Take a minute to look up imposter syndrome online or type #impostersyndrome into Instagram or Twitter and you'll find thousands of posts about it. There are message boards, news articles, personal experiences – I'm not the only one talking about this.

Finally, take time to reflect after reading a chapter or trying a strategy. Reflection helps us refine our thoughts, evaluate our capabilities and set realistic goals, so we keep track of our progress and build confidence in our ability to succeed. We learn much more from our experiences when we reflect on what we've done.

To gain the most from the strategies you try, make notes. Buy yourself a notebook to use alongside this book. Writing things down allows you to reflect; it is a great motivator and you can look back and see how you've done. I love a notebook – there's something about it that feels special – but if you prefer using your phone you could write in the notes section, whichever is easiest and you're most likely to do. This will help you commit to what you're doing and keep the strategy in mind.

Making notes will give you a chance to gain new perspectives and consider an alternative way of thinking about yourself and your achievements. If you accepted the theory, you wouldn't need this book as you know some of the arguments already, you're just choosing to ignore them. There's evidence of your success all around you and it's time you started seeing it too.

While you can't yet be sure that my way will work, you *can* be sure that what you're currently doing is definitely not working. Think of the time, effort and energy you're putting into keeping this secret. It's time to try something new and you may as well give this a proper chance. You deserve to enjoy your life again. I know I can make that happen if you take on board and try out everything in this book.

You will feel uncomfortable at first, but don't worry. Growth isn't meant to be comfortable; I'm pushing you out of autopilot and into uncharted territory. You will learn new skills and they will stretch you. It will be like learning a new language: the words will sound strange and clunky at first, but over time, with regular practice and hard work, you will begin to improve and feel less self-conscious.

When I work with people I find that their viewpoint changes and they're able to think differently fairly quickly as long as they're ready and motivated to change. However, it can take a bit longer for their feelings to catch up. It's a matter of, 'I know it, but I don't feel it yet.' Give yourself time; you've had a fixed view of yourself for many years. It won't change overnight and you need to allow your feelings to catch up with your new thinking.

Have faith in the process and hang on to the hope that there is an alternative viewpoint. I promise it will be worth it. Hard as it might be to believe, you're not so far away from the life you want.

Before you continue, take a minute to think about your reasons for change. What do you want to gain from this book? What do you want to be different? Think about the impact this could have. Write this commitment on the first page of your notebook or in your phone notes.

Commitment

I ....
commit to reading and trying out every strategy in this book.

I will give this a proper chance; I will talk about imposter syndrome and reflect on everything I learn.

My top three hopes for the book are:

1 . ...

2 . ...

3 . ...

Signed

. . . .

PART I

UNDERSTANDING
IMPOSTER
SYNDROME

Chapter 1
What is imposter syndrome?

'The more you know about imposter syndrome the better your chance of beating it. Keep your friends close and your enemies closer...'

By the end of this chapter you should:
- Understand that imposter syndrome affects lots of people, at different times in their lives
- Recognize the negative impact of imposter syndrome
- Begin to identify which competence type (or types) you fall into

I'm so pleased you're giving this a try and I promise you will find it worthwhile. Before I tackle the causes and symptoms of imposter syndrome, I want to give you a bit of background and explain the science behind it. The more you know about imposter syndrome the better your chance of beating it. Keep your friends close and your enemies closer...

Imposter syndrome was first described by two clinical psychologists – Dr Pauline Clance and Dr Suzanne Imes – in 1978. They noticed that their female students were full of doubt about their abilities and worried about continuing their successes.

One female student stated: 'I was convinced that I would be discovered as a phony when I took my comprehensive doctoral examination. I thought the final test had come. In one way, I was somewhat relieved at this prospect because the pretense would finally be over. I was shocked when my chairman told me that my answers were excellent and that my paper was one of the best he had seen in his entire career.'

Together, Clance and Imes conducted interviews with 150 highly successful women (students and professionals), and found that 'despite their earned degrees, scholastic honors, high achievement on standardized tests, praise and professional recognition from colleagues and respected authorities, these women do not experience an internal sense of success. They consider themselves to be "imposters".'

As a result of their research, they coined the term 'imposter phenomenon', a condition in which people believe they are not worthy of success and have a persistent belief in their lack of intelligence, skills or competence. They referred to an 'internal experience of intellectual phoniness'; these women had achieved success, but found it uncomfortable, fearing they had arrived there by mistake or through luck. As a result, they experienced intense feelings that their achievements were undeserved and had an overwhelming fear of everything falling apart, despite evidence to the contrary.

Imposter syndrome is technically not a syndrome as the thoughts and feelings of being an imposter that people experience occur in certain situations and are not present all the time.

Who does it affect?

Imposter syndrome was originally believed to affect a narrow sample of high-achieving women, but psychologists now recognize that it is far more widespread. It particularly affects those who are successful and bright and those who have no obvious reason to feel insecure – especially those who find it hard to internalize their achievements or recognize the good parts of themselves. The syndrome has a deep impact on many aspects of their day-to-day lives – their jobs, relationships and friendships as well as their confidence as parents. Despite this their struggles are often invisible to others.

About 70 per cent of people have felt some degree of imposter syndrome and it is something almost everyone can relate to. It can harm people from all walks of life, affects both men and women and occurs across different cultures. It affects those in academic settings – undergrads, mature students, PhD students and even professors. Imposter syndrome is common in all work settings, especially highly competitive business cultures in which performance is constantly under scrutiny and competition is encouraged. It is also experienced by those who are self-employed, particularly those who work on a project basis and have to actively 'win' work. It can creep into personal lives and can affect relationships. It might make you feel that you are not as good as your friends and make you question why they want to spend time with you. Or you could be the husband who feels his wife will realize the mistake she has made in marrying him, or the working mum who feels a failure because she can't make time for all her children's school events.

I think of it as a problem that has its roots in simply not feeling good enough. Instead of seeing this and working to overcome it, your brain concludes that you must be an imposter. The mind-trap of imposter syndrome then makes it impossible to revise this belief.

The varying degrees of imposter syndrome

Imposter syndrome runs on a continuum from an occasional worry that you're not up to the task to full-blown fears of being 'found out'. It can cause chronic self-doubt, fear and shame, making it hard to enjoy life or to live in the moment. Trying to pass as something you're not feels incredibly stressful. It can be exhausting keeping the 'show' going. It can also affect you physically with bursts of adrenaline, increased heart rate, a creeping sense of dread or general tension. These thoughts and sensations exacerbate the problem, adding to your feelings of inadequacy and colouring how you think and behave.

The syndrome can affect people at different life stages and can increase or decrease in severity, depending on what's going on in your life. It may occur in just one area of your life, or in specific situations. It might be a thought that only comes up when you're doing something new, or it might manifest as a sudden worry that overcomes you at the worst possible moments. Maybe you've been pushing to be perfect for so long that you no longer see what's driving that push. Or perhaps you have a nagging doubt always in the background making you feel insecure, prone to procrastination and unable to reach your full potential. Some people, such as James, can be affected all the time and this can lead to a terrifying existence.

Every time James walks through the door of his big house he feels he is intruding, that at any moment someone will knock on the door and tell him that this house is not his. He will be told he doesn't deserve to live there and that his life there has all been a mistake.

James is 45. He is a successful businessman who has helped to found two thriving companies in the tech sector. He has two great children and a loving wife. He seems to have everything. In the eyes of his friends and colleagues, James is a success story – someone to live up to. Yet James feels his life is a fraud. He has got where he is through luck and at any moment this will be exposed and his career will be over.

James lives in fear: fear of being found out, and fear of failing himself and his family. This fear affects almost every moment of his working day. He lives in a constant state of anxiety and has little joy in his work. He finds it hard to enjoy his successes, despite the praise he receives from others. He sees the negatives before the positives and is overcritical of his projects. He looks enviously at other businesses and colleagues and wonders why life is so easy for them and so difficult for him.

He has often come close to sabotaging his career. He once resigned from a business in which he was achieving great things to join a smaller business in a lesser role. He felt he was not good enough and was failing badly – it was only a matter of time before he would be forced out. When he resigned his boss was shocked to discover that James felt he was failing and couldn't keep up. He was a valued member of staff who had been making a great contribution to the business. His boss talked him out of leaving and immediately hired an assistant to help with the workload. That's how highly he rated James.

James drinks too much. He drinks to numb anxiety. He drinks to dismiss the memories of his turbulent childhood and he drinks to push away the highs and lows of everyday life. The effects of this drinking compound his problem. As a result of his heavy morning head, he feels a fraud at home as well as at work. He worries that he could be a better husband and a better father. He could be more present, more kind, more loving.

James is finding it more difficult to push his feelings to the back of his mind as he gets older. He has more responsibilities now – a family to look after, staff who depend on his decisions for their livelihood. When he was younger he pushed on regardless, despite the nagging doubts and insecurities. Now he feels he is at breaking point. Only the support and love of his wife keeps him from falling apart. He has dreams of running away, of burying himself in mounds of pillowy nothingness. The saddest thing is that no one knows that James feels this away. He pushes away those who worry about him and refuses to let them help. He can't see the fulfilling, happy life he could have if he let them in.

When you're at the extreme end of imposter syndrome as James is it can have an incredibly negative effect on your life. When you try to ignore the problem, its impact is corrosive. Imposter syndrome prevents people believing in themselves and the more they achieve the worse they feel. Unable to fully own their accomplishments or good traits, they remain disconnected from all the good things they do. This makes it impossible for them to update their view and build a sense of self-worth or an inner measure of how they're doing. For many others the effect is less extreme.

Whether you are like James – whose confidence and self-belief is constantly undermined by imposter syndrome – or it has a more subtle impact on you, it is a problem that no one should ignore.

The negative impact of imposter syndrome

Research has begun to show just how harmful imposter syndrome can be. As well as daily fear and distress it has a whole host of other negative effects on your behaviour, and on how you feel physically and emotionally. For instance, you might wake up feeling anxious, which makes you more likely to have anxious thoughts. You then might start to feel this anxiety as a physical sensation, with increased heart rate or nervous stomach. This physical discomfort can then make it harder for you to focus on your work, causing you to procrastinate. But this link between thoughts, feelings and behaviours is cyclical – they all feed in to each other. As you read this next section, consider which symptoms and effects apply to you. These will be good motivators for change!

I'm sure it's no surprise to discover that there are links between imposter syndrome and low self-esteem. If you believe you're lacking in some way, you are much more likely to undervalue your achievements and alter your goals and ambitions to reflect your insecurity. Throw in perfectionism and a fear of failure and it's no wonder you find it so difficult to build an inner measure of how you're doing. This belief also feeds into day-to-day life; when you feel less confident you worry about your capabilities and this can inhibit you and prevent you succeeding. When you don't achieve what you set out to do, this proves that your original fears about not being good enough were justified, causing your confidence to drop even further.

Overwork, avoidance, self-criticism and self-doubt are a toxic combination, leading to feelings of shame and inadequacy. Insecurity can show itself as self-doubt or it can switch you into defensive mode, driving you to push others away, as well as making it harder for you to see a different view. The constant stress means you're running on adrenaline and are always on edge, which can result in tiredness, tension and a loss of motivation. Physical manifestations of the problem can also emerge – migraine, back pain and autoimmune disorders. The syndrome can cause depression and anxiety and lead to emotional and physical exhaustion.

Imposter syndrome has long-lasting effects on careers, undermining professional adaptability. Fear of failure means that students drop out of university, people abandon their dreams, say no to promotions or, like James, apply for jobs that are beneath them. The imposter doesn't see that failure is a normal part of life.

The knock-on effect is that imposters are often not satisfied by their work or career path and may at times feel stuck, while at the same time being more concerned about keeping their current position than pushing on to tackle a new challenge that might expose them as a fraud.

Most – although not all – imposters are people pleasers, constantly trying to adapt themselves, putting others' needs first and not thinking about their own. It's hard to feel close to others when you don't like yourself very much. Trying to be something to everyone means you have nothing left for yourself and can make you feel disconnected from your relationships. You may feel that no one really knows you, that you are misunderstood and alone and this prevents you feeling close to the people you care about.

Or the opposite can happen; you become controlling towards others. When you set yourself excessively high standards and don't trust yourself, this can make it very difficult to trust others. You may watch everyone closely, be overcritical if people don't do things your way and find it hard to delegate. This micromanagement and inability to let go leaves you with not just your work, but everyone else's too. It also makes you pretty unpopular and will not get the best out of your team.

Many imposters go through life with a fairly negative impression of themselves, at least when they are experiencing a period of imposter syndrome. This limits what you do, stops you trying new things and prevents you gaining more experience. It becomes harder to achieve your goals, to learn from your mistakes and therefore to grow and improve. As a result you rarely experience what it's like to feel good about your work, to properly acknowledge your successes, or discover the excitement of learning and succeeding. This prevents you getting to know your true self and building a realistic internal measure of how you're doing, which means you don't experience the inner stability and calm that comes from acknowledging these things.

Why does it happen?

Imposter syndrome can be triggered by any achievement or approval-related task or as a result of feeling insecure about your knowledge or skills, particularly when you work in a competitive atmosphere and when responsibilities increase.

It tends to be exacerbated during times of transition or change, or when you are faced with new challenges – such as a new job, project or being accepted into higher education. This pushes you out of your comfort zone into new routines and puts you under increased scrutiny. There are new codes to learn, a new role to play and a new way of being. There is also a lot more you don't know – from how to be and how to act, to where the bathrooms and coffee machine are – and these periods tend to involve more evaluation and a heavier workload as you get up to speed. But changes and challenges are not the only things that have an impact. You can have been in a job for a long time and still experience the syndrome, if you are unable to update your view of yourself, see yourself as capable and take on board your achievements.

The syndrome can also occur when you feel different from the core group you are part of. If, for example, you are one of the few women in a male-dominated sector or someone of a different race or sexuality and don't match the dominant group, this can make you feel illegitimate or fake despite your qualifications and accomplishments. You may feel that you have a lot to live up to and this brings even greater expectations. You're representing not just yourself but a social group, and if people have a negative opinion of your group, the pressure can increase even more. It can also lead to thoughts that you're only here thanks to positive discrimination, so you dismiss your success.

Traditional gender norms can also have an impact. There are still far fewer women than men holding senior positions and although this is changing, not that long ago women's main life goal was to get married and have a baby. Even now a woman's successful career is sometimes seen as being at the expense of the family, something that doesn't feature in men's lives. The conflicting messages about achievement can make it difficult to internalize success. These norms also place a greater expectation on men. Society values men who demonstrate high levels of competence, and pressure can make you question whether you can meet expectations and worry that you are not measuring up.

The mind-trap of imposter syndrome

Imposter syndrome normally occurs when there is a tension between two views – yours and what you believe others expect of you. Or the tension could be between the standards you set yourself and how you assess yourself as doing. When the image you have of yourself – a general sense of not being good enough – doesn't match what others see, you conclude that they must have an inflated idea of your abilities, making you feel a fraud.

If you don't perform to the highest standards, this leads to feelings of shame and anxiety and you wrongly conclude that this reveals something essential about your lack of ability and talent. When faced with a new challenge anxiety increases; because you lack belief in yourself you immediately fear that you might not be able to rise to the challenge. Fear of failure and self-doubt drive the cycle – if you fail you're sure to be found out.

The high standards you set yourself are a large part of the problem, as is the negative internal voice you use to motivate yourself. You expect that you need to be the best and do everything flawlessly in your career, relationships and personal life.

This pressure to achieve then goes one of two ways. You either overwork and drive for perfection to reach those lofty standards. Or you do the opposite, grinding to a halt, procrastinating and paralysed by self-doubt. This is often followed by a belated frenzy of work to meet a deadline; you'll do anything to avoid these uncomfortable feelings.

Despite all this negative thinking success often follows, but rather than celebrate this, the overworker interprets achievement as the result of unsustainable levels of effort. The dedication and work they put in is much greater than anyone else's. The procrastinator sees success as due to luck, knowing that they had made a last-minute effort and were winging it.

Based on your interpretation your response is understandable: if you really are a fraud then you need to do these things to ensure you are not found out. Everything you do is aimed at stopping others finding out the 'truth'. In the short-term your coping strategies make you feel better, safe, with a chance that you won't be discovered. But if your beliefs about yourself are wrong and you are not an imposter, as I suspect, then these behaviours are part of the problem.

What is your competence type?

When you think about this cycle, it's clear that your definition of competence has an impact on what you expect of yourself. You have an idea in your head of how well you should do, setting yourself incredibly high and unsustainable standards. If there is a discrepancy between your actual and ideal standards of success, then you disregard what others say and this strengthens the feeling of being a fraud.

Dr Valerie Young, an expert on imposter syndrome and author of *The Secret Thoughts of Successful Women: Why Capable People Suffer from the Impostor Syndrome and How to Thrive in Spite of It*, discovered that imposters experience failure-related shame in different ways, because they don't all define competence in the same way. She uncovered five 'competence types', internal rules that people with imposter syndrome generally follow: the Perfectionist, the Natural Genius, the Soloist, the Expert and the Superwoman/man.

Have a read through all five and see which you recognize – you may find you fit into more than one category. Understanding which category you fall into can be really helpful. Once you are aware of this, it gives you a better chance of understanding the patterns you fall into and then you can make a conscious choice to change.

The Perfectionist

Perfectionism and imposter syndrome often go hand in hand and this is the most common type of imposter. As Young writes, 'The Perfectionist's primary focus is on "how" something is done. This includes how the work is conducted and how it turns out.'

Perfectionists set excessively high standards for themselves and believe they should deliver a perfect performance 100 per cent of the time, thereby creating a cycle where their best efforts are never good enough, even when they reach 99 per cent of their goals.

Perfectionists have a very specific vision of what they want and a very precise plan to reach it. They believe that there is a right way and a wrong way to do things – there's no room for a detour or a different outcome. They are never content with anything unless it is of the highest possible quality and, rather than celebrating the things they did well, they tend to focus on the areas where they could have done better.

Perfectionists imagine that others hold them to these standards and often measure friends, family and work colleagues by them too. Sadly, no one can possibly live up to them. Perfectionists tend to believe that 'if you want something done right you must do it yourself' and as a result find it difficult to trust in others' abilities, fearing that 'they won't do it properly'. Perfectionists may also find it difficult if they are not in control.

If you're a Perfectionist, when you don't do things perfectly (as no one can), you experience self-doubt and worry, ashamed that you are not measuring up and have 'failed'. This drive for perfection and fear of failure can leave you deliberating over micro details, either procrastinating or overworking. It might also mean you give up on things too quickly if you find them difficult or can't do them perfectly. When perfection is the aim, everything is always going to fall short, and success is seldom satisfying.

The Natural Genius

Young's second competence type is the Natural Genius: 'the Natural Genius cares "how" and "when" accomplishments happen'. They set their internal bar impossibly high, just like Perfectionists, but rather than judging themselves by an unrealistically high standard they judge themselves on whether they get things right at the first try. Young found that for this group, '*true* competence means having inherent intelligence and ability'. There is no room for development. When they can't get something right on the first try, struggle to master a new skill or take too long (by their own judgement) to do something, this evokes feelings of shame and leaves them feeling like an imposter.

As such, Natural Geniuses strive to master any new skill quickly and with little effort. They believe that if they have to work hard at something then they must not be very good at it. Competence means being able to do things quickly and easily and if they need to learn something new development should be effortless. When this isn't the case they believe they must be doing badly. They are often overly optimistic about how much they can get done in the time available and when progress is slower than expected they feel disappointed in themselves.

If you are a Natural Genius you probably got by in school without studying, but gave up at the first sign of a challenge if you weren't top of the class. As a result you have little practice at perseverance – a necessary life skill. When you start doing something new and have difficulty achieving it, you immediately think something is wrong with you, rather than seeing you haven't given yourself enough time. Setbacks completely throw you and you avoid taking risks in case you fail.

The Soloist

The Soloist defines competence as being able to do something on their own and believes that achievement only counts if it is unassisted. Young found that 'the Soloist cares mostly about "who" completes the task' – to do well, they believe they must be able to do it on their own. Soloists typically turn down help so they can prove their worth as an individual, and if they need help they see it as a sign of failure, which evokes feelings of shame and triggers imposter feelings.

Soloists value independence over everything else, including their own needs. They are unwilling to ask for support even if a project is not going well or the sheer amount of work needed to make it succeed is killing them. When they struggle or feel stuck it can lead to procrastination to avoid admitting 'defeat'.

If you are a Soloist you tend to think you need to work out and do everything on your own. You view projects, accomplishments or ideas that were derived in conjunction with someone else as not being your own achievement. Asking for help is a sign of weakness and you fear it might reveal your incompetence.

The Expert

Young's fourth competence type is the Expert. As Young explains, 'the Expert is the knowledge version of the Perfectionist'. They need to know it all and believe true competence means knowing absolutely everything. 'Here the primary concern is on "what" and "how much" you know or can do.' They believe if they were really clever they would already know everything they need to know to master a challenge before they even start. They do not feel satisfied until they have a comprehensive understanding of a subject.

When Experts don't know the answer to every single question, they blame themselves for being incompetent instead of acknowledging their skill gaps and working to fill them. They deeply fear being exposed as inexperienced or lacking knowledge, and endlessly seek out more information, which is often just another disguise for procrastination.

If they don't fit every single requirement in a job description, Experts are unlikely to apply. They may think they have somehow tricked their employer into hiring them and imagine that their employer expects them to know more than they do. They often falter before beginning a job or task and even if they've been in their role for some time they feel like they still don't know enough.

If you are an Expert you'll have a degree – maybe more than one. Despite completing multiple courses it's never enough and there's always something more you feel you need to know. This drives you to gain as much knowledge and as many skills as possible, believing that there must be a certain threshold of experience that is needed to be successful or considered competent and skilled (rather than learning as you go). You continuously hunt for new information, which can sometimes get in the way of completing tasks and projects.

The Superwoman/man

The Supers push themselves to work harder than everyone else. Young finds this competence type 'measures competence based on "how many" roles they can both juggle and excel in' – boss, colleague, partner, parent, friend, volunteer, host. They expect that they should be able to fulfil them all perfectly and with ease. If they fall short in any of their self-designated roles, they feel shame because they believe they should be able to handle everything.

Supers set unrealistically high standards in every area and are, like the Perfectionist, on turbocharge. Young differentiates the two by how they interpret their competence, with the Super defining it 'based on their ability to perform perfectly in multiple roles vs. the Perfectionist who cares predominantly about their work, career or studies'.

Supers often excel in all areas, because they push themselves so hard and want to juggle all of their roles perfectly. This can lead to living overextended lives. Trying to do everything at home alongside succeeding at work and never allowing themselves a break, Supers are addicted to the validation that comes from working rather than the work itself. This overload of pressure will eventually result in burnout, which can affect physical and mental health, and relationships with others.

You're a Super if you measure yourself not just on how well you do things but also on how many things you can juggle at one time. You believe you can do it all and are unable to say 'no' even if you're struggling to keep up with everything. You have an unrealistic view of how much is possible and are switched on all the time, unable to enjoy downtime or non-achievement-based activities.

Before you go…

Think about the following and write your thoughts in your notes.

- Which imposter types fit with your ideas of competence?
- What impact does this have on how you do things?
- What negative effects is imposter syndrome having on your life?

Chapter 2
The survival strategy of self-doubt

'Just because you worry you are an imposter, it doesn't mean you are one. Your feelings are not facts.'

By the end of this chapter you should:

- Understand where feelings come from and how they influence our day-to-day lives and decisions
- See that feelings should not be interpreted as evidence or facts
- Learn some facts to help you cope with imposter tendencies

Feelings are important and I'm all for trusting them. I wouldn't be much of a psychologist if I told you otherwise! Emotions guide your beliefs and the meaning you give to things in life. They provide us with information and communicate our inner worlds to others – they are an indicator to us of what's going on, they help us process information and they act as a warning signal when we're not feeling so good. Guilt helps us right a wrong; grief allows us to get over a loss; love brings us closer to others. Emotions are an essential part of who we are and how we survive. But, and it's a *big* but, they are not always accurate – and fear can be a particularly tricky emotion.

Unfortunately, imposter syndrome is all about fear. Fear of being found out, fear of failure, fear of not being good enough and chronic self-doubt. To understand why fear can be problematic we first need to take a trip back in time and consider how our brains are wired and the original function of our fear response.

The human brain is the product of many millions of years of evolution based around one simple goal: survival. To survive, early humans needed a highly responsive threat system – this is called the amygdala and is still part of our brains now.

Our brains work a bit like computers, constantly processing information received through our senses, and the amygdala is automatically triggered when we feel fear, anxiety or stress, setting off a fight or flight reaction in our bodies.

This all happens in an instant, before we're even aware of it. In evolutionary terms, this speed makes it an amazing threat detector, but the speed of reaction means that it can sometimes be triggered unnecessarily – in the same way as an oversensitive burglar alarm. When potential dangers were life-threatening it was better to be safe than sorry, but now that we're neither hunting nor hunted, this very primitive part of the brain can sometimes work against us.

As we evolved, we became conscious of ourselves in a way that animals are not. Our brains began to think in new ways and develop new abilities, such as being able to use attention and imagination to think, plan, reason and reflect. This has allowed us to do some amazing things – build cities, discover new lands and develop technology – but it can also cause us problems.

We can worry about the future, ruminate on the past, compare ourselves negatively to others or be self-critical, and our amygdala is so primitive that it cannot distinguish between a real threat (such as meeting a tiger) and a perceived threat (such as the fear that you are an imposter). This means that the fight-or-flight response can be activated when we don't need it, putting us on high alert when there's nothing to fight or flee from except our thoughts.

Our brains were ideal for their original purpose – surviving a life in the wild – but they weren't designed for modern life. Left to their own devices, our brains will consistently misinterpret the signals of the twenty-first century.

Having such a sensitive threat detector means that fear-based reasoning is not always accurate. It's brilliant at getting us out of trouble, for example when a car comes too quickly towards us and we run to get out of the way. But it's not so helpful when our feelings are not based on accurate information or when there is no real threat.

Think about being at the cinema watching a scary movie. You know you're in the cinema, safely watching a film, but that doesn't stop you feeling terrified and reacting to everything that happens on screen. In this situation – unlike imposter syndrome – you *know* absolutely that you are not in danger and yet you still feel the response.

Imposters fear being found out or not being good enough so strongly that they do not question their fear. If what you believe is true, then you're right to be scared: being found out, failing, the humiliation that comes with what you imagine – these are terrifying.

But what if you're not right? This is impossible for you to see when the fear response is so strong. It is shouting that you're in danger so loudly, that you can't see anything else. Add the rush of physical sensations this triggers – increased heart rate and breathing, tension and heat – and it's almost impossible to look rationally at what's going on. There's no chance to look at all the information or carefully weigh things up and then decide what to do.

Feelings are not facts

What confuses the situation further is that our emotions are intrinsically linked to our thoughts and behaviour. Feelings can trigger certain thoughts and reactions just as certain actions and thoughts can trigger feelings. They are all connected. Our feelings colour our thoughts and shape them: feeling anxious might prompt you to fear you're not up to the task, while thinking you're not up to the task will prompt you to feel fear.

Fear puts an anxious filter on everything we do. I'm sure you've experienced this: on the days when you're feeling good you glimpse how well you're doing, but soon fear overrides the positives. Nothing dramatic has changed, but the feeling is different.

There's a fine line between feelings and facts. Our feelings can trick us into believing that things are worse than they are, but feelings are only one piece of the puzzle. You need to use your thoughts and experience to see the full picture. It's only when you put them all together that you can see clearly what's going on.

Imagine you had a chance to interview people before they competed in a race. Would you predict that the person who *felt* most confident that they were going to win would in fact be the first to cross the finish line? If they looked you in the eye and said, 'I feel really confident, I feel I'm definitely going to win,' would you back them without any further questions?

I'd find their confidence convincing, but if they were basing their confidence only on a feeling, I wouldn't trust them fully. Personally, I'd want to know a bit more – how well they've prepared for this race, what their recent form has been like, how well they've been running, and what their coach thinks. I would want to know the facts, I'd want more evidence. I'm not going to back someone simply because they *feel* they will win.

Yet this is what you're doing if you rely on your feelings as your most accurate source of information. When it comes to imposter syndrome you *know* you're an imposter, but everyone else sees something different. You have a catalogue of achievements, but you don't count them. Your belief that you are an imposter is not based on evidence you can show someone – there are no huge muck-ups or epic fails – it's based on a feeling. But just because you worry you are an imposter, it doesn't mean you are one. Your feelings are not facts. You need to listen to your feelings, but do not treat them as more important than all other information. It's important to use your head *and* your heart.

Hooked on a feeling

Let's put this in the context of what's going on in your life. If you think back to the last chapter, you've learned that imposter syndrome tends to be triggered by any achievement or approval-related task. Doing something difficult or trying something new pushes you out of your comfort zone. When faced with a new challenge anxiety increases and it's natural to experience some fear.

This discomfort is something we all experience; it's a normal response – the feeling you have when you say 'ugh' with a crinkled-up nose, slightly gritted teeth and a reaction in your stomach. It is caused in part by uncertainty. Can I do this? Am I the right person for the job? These questions are understandably daunting.

The big question is: why do some people conclude from this that they are an imposter, while others can experience this discomfort and think little of it?

The answer goes back to how you *interpret* that feeling of discomfort. When imposters experience it they recognize the feeling as meaning they are a fraud, falsely believing that if they were good enough or ready for this challenge they wouldn't feel like this and imagining that confident people feel differently.

The reality is that these things are difficult for everyone; we all feel uncertain of ourselves at times, but imposters misinterpret this rather than recognizing it as normal and part of being human. As an imposter you think that not only are you not good enough for the job, but you have faked your way in there and don't have the goods to back it up, a bit like Poppy.

Poppy couldn't believe it. She'd been given the book deal she'd always dreamed of, with an amazing publishing house. Finally, here was the opportunity she'd been waiting for. Yet as the news began to sink in a feeling of dread crept over her, replacing the momentary happiness. How was she going to write a book? What were they thinking agreeing to this when she had zero experience of writing anything? It's all very well getting a publishing deal, she thought to herself, but now I've got to actually write something for people to read.

She looked at the other books on the market – their writing flowed beautifully, the content was so engaging; she knew there was no way she could do something like that. How had she managed to convince them she could? Nerves filled her body, which suddenly felt on high alert. She wasn't a proper author, she'd just had an idea for a book and now she had to back it up. This was well beyond her capabilities. Didn't they realize she was just an average person who had enough trouble staying on top of her online weekly shop and washing pile, without throwing a book into the mix?

All her friends were delighted for her and so impressed, but that just made her feel worse. However much she tried to explain to them that the whole thing was just good timing and a lot of luck, they didn't listen. When she tried to explain how anxious she felt, they refused to take her seriously, telling her she was worrying over nothing. If they only knew the internal struggles she was going through. But hard as she tried, she couldn't make them understand. In the end she gave up trying to convince them. If she'd had her way, she wouldn't have told anyone her news; it meant there'd just be more people to witness the whole thing falling apart as it undoubtedly would.

Poppy started the book and the voice grew quieter, but she still couldn't shift the nagging doubt that this was going to be a disaster. Somehow she met her deadline. She felt a wave of relief when she sent it off to her editor, but when the books arrived boxed up on her doorstep, instead of feeling excited she felt a heavy weight. What if no one likes it? It doesn't mean anything if you write a book and it doesn't sell. In the run-up to the launch, she hardly slept: she thought the reviews were going to be terrible and that everyone would see what a fraud she was.

Slowly the reviews trickled in and the book had a really positive response. Poppy's agent called her to tell her how pleased the publishers were and asked if she would like to meet them to talk about a second book. Her whole body became tense and heat rushed through her. This book had clearly been a fluke; she felt physically sick at the prospect of having to go through this again – there was no chance she would be so lucky the second time around.

To anyone but Poppy, it would be clear that the book had a positive response because it was good. It would be pretty difficult to fool everyone into believing this if it wasn't true, but right from the start Poppy misinterprets her feeling of dread and her level of fear becomes so high that it changes how she sees things. Instead of looking rationally at what is going on, she predicts that it's going to be a disaster and her internal voice becomes very negative. Every time she hits a goal – meeting the deadline, getting good reviews, being asked to write a second book – there's a chance for her to change her view, but she prevents this happening by moving the goalposts. As a result, none of it counts for her, she feels no better and the cycle continues as she begins her next book feeling just as terrified.

This is why imposter syndrome can be so difficult to change; you base your conclusions on how you *feel*, rather than on anything you have done. Your thoughts are skewed by this feeling, making you ignore any information that doesn't fit your view and collect dodgy evidence to support it. No matter how many projects you complete or how capable others think you are, your thoughts about yourself do not match up.

Of course, there is some truth in these fears; they're understandable, so it can be hard to see that this is imposter syndrome in action. I think of this in terms of surveys: if you surveyed 100 people before they started a new job how would they feel? I'd guess 98 per cent would feel nervous. It's not ridiculous to want to do a good job or to feel under more pressure when you are promoted and have a bigger team that relies on you. But your reaction is disproportionate – the level of fear is too high and does not reflect the true situation.

This interpretation increases anxiety, setting off the fight-or-flight response so your thoughts become coloured by fear and the physical anxiety provides confirmation that something *must* be wrong. This leaves you stuck with a belief regardless of logic – it's something you just *know* even though it's not based on any factual information.

This is further compounded by the fact that you only hear what's going on in your head, forgetting that you're not the only one who feels like this. Unable to hear the internal monologues in other people's heads, you wrongly presume that because they look all right from the outside they must be keeping it all together. In reality your fears and doubts are likely to be very similar. It's just that everyone is keeping them a secret!

What's the alternative?

Confident people do feel this discomfort and do experience some of the same fears. But they come to a different conclusion and this allows them to override their feelings. Instead of interpreting their discomfort as meaning that they are imposters, they take a very different path.

They might recognize the discomfort as a fear associated with doing something new and stepping out of their comfort zone. The discomfort is caused by anxiety and non-imposters recognize it as just that, seeing it as a sign that they're unsure or they worry that they won't do well – again, all very human and all very normal. They may also recognize that anxiety is not all bad and make use of its good elements. It gears you up for a change, keeps you on your toes and makes you more alert. Or they might see that even if everything doesn't work out, they'll learn something from doing it.

This means that their anxiety doesn't increase further so the fight or flight reaction is not set off. Confident people can then think more clearly about what to do next and how best to handle things. They might talk to someone about it or find out more about what they're expected to do. This allows them to look at their experience and knowledge and reassure themselves that they can take on the task. They may also recall a previous time when they felt like this when everything had turned out fine. They experience the same feelings, but interpret them very differently.

People in this group know that to a certain extent they *are* imposters. It's just that they don't see this as a problem. They understand that there is a certain amount of bluff involved in life (and love), especially at the beginning of a new job or challenge. No one starts a job knowing everything about it and in any relationship you share different parts of yourself; very few people see all of you. The difference is that confident people are happy to trust their instincts and ability to learn. They trust that they can grow into the person they need to be.

We are all imposters – everyone wings it a bit – but those who believe they are 'imposters' see this as a problem rather than a normal reaction to not knowing something. Their belief that they are an imposter is so strong that they are unable to dismiss their feelings; it blinds them to any other information, so they are unable to take on board their achievements. This prevents them from seeing and internalizing their log of experience so, unlike a more confident person, they have nothing to fall back on and draw from. The next time they're in a similar situation, it seems that nothing has changed. Add to this the fact that an imposter's negative self-talk is anything but reassuring and that the feelings they experience in response to this discomfort only serve to confirm that they are right – they are not up to the task.

It's our response to the discomfort that is key! To move forward you need to see that the problem is not you, it's your *interpretation* of this feeling – don't use a feeling as information or evidence for how you're doing. This discomfort is a normal reaction and something everyone experiences – *not* a sign that you are an imposter.

I know you're not yet there in terms of *knowing* this, but for now I want you to take a leap of faith and let yourself explore this new idea – what if you have been misinterpreting this feeling? That it's a normal feeling that everyone experiences? What if you're wrong and you're not an imposter? What if you're where you are in your life because you deserve to be?

I also want you to start to notice that feeling of discomfort. When you recognize it and see that it's part of the imposter cycle, it begins to lose some of its power. As we go through the book I'll share lots of strategies to help you manage it, but for now simply seeing it in action is a brilliant first step.

Repeat after me:

- Feelings are not facts
- Feeling discomfort doesn't mean I can't do something
- Anxiety is a normal reaction

Chapter 3
Why me?

'Looking back at your history
is not about blaming anyone,
it's about understanding
yourself better.'

By the end of this chapter you should:
- Begin to see that certain beliefs and personality types can predispose you to imposter syndrome
- Be able to identify the beliefs that may be having an impact on you and understand how and when you might have formed them
- Start to challenge those beliefs

I hope you're starting to see that your feelings do not mark you out as different. We all experience insecurity and lack confidence at times. No one knows it all and feeling uncomfortable doesn't mean that you don't deserve success or that you are any less capable, intelligent or worthy.

Where did these beliefs that you are less capable or worthy than others come from? When did this feeling of not being good enough begin? To answer this question, we need to look back at your history and unpick how you got to this point. This is something I do in therapy to build a fuller picture of what's going on. I like to find out more about what growing up was like, your parents' expectations, your relationships and your personality. This information provides clues to how someone formed their beliefs and why they think as they do.

Nature or nurture?

Our beliefs and impressions of the world and our view of ourselves and others are formed in childhood. Family environment, family dynamics and the way our parents raised us combine with our personality and our experience of the world to shape our belief system and give us a sense of who we are as a person. This means that what you learned as a child influences how you see and experience things now, and these childhood experiences shape your approach to life.

Until I had children I really underestimated the part that personality plays in development. But when you spend time with babies you quickly realize that personality traits play a big part in how you interact with the world. Many psychologists who specialize in personality traits believe that there are five basic dimensions (often referred to as the Big Five) – extraversion, agreeableness, openness, conscientiousness and neuroticism. Research suggests that if you are naturally more prone to anxiety and worrying and have perfectionist tendencies (classified as neuroticism) you are more likely to experience imposter fears.

Nature and nurture are not separate – each has an impact on the other. Your personality type interacts with your experiences and has an effect on the world's response to you. If you are an easy-going baby who sleeps well and smiles a lot, your parents will be more relaxed with you and you'll be unfazed by new situations. You'll be handed round, taken to new places and the response from the world will be positive – strangers will smile at you in the street and life will run smoothly.

You'll experience a very different reaction if you are a more nervous baby who cries a lot and never sleeps. Your parents may be more stressed in their interactions with you and your world will be a bit smaller as it will be difficult to take you anywhere and strangers will tend to give you a wide berth. The world will look and feel quite different, depending on which baby you are. So personality not only changes your world directly, it also changes it indirectly. But nurture clearly plays a role too.

When we're born our brains aren't fully developed and we come into the world ready to collect information from our environment. Children really are like little sponges. They absorb information from their surroundings and pick up on everything that's going on – even when you don't intend them to. I witness this on a daily basis, hearing my children repeating my own words. My son gives his sisters a stern talking to and tells them that all this noise is giving him a headache. Or my daughter tells me she doesn't want to hear a song again as it's 'driving her crazy'.

Our brains are belief-making machines; they are constantly linking up ideas and forming opinions about the world. You see a bird and are told it's a bird, you see a flower and are told it's the colour red; with repeated reinforcement through repetition and exposure we soon learn what birds and the colour red look like.

When we are children our thinking has not yet matured, so these ideas are taken as 'the truth'. We tend to accept what we are told and conclude that this is an accurate view of the world. We rarely think that others might be wrong or ill-informed and we have very limited opportunities to check out these ideas, unlike when we're older. We can't use a computer or research an idea in other ways and we don't think to ask others about it or have a chance to hear alternative viewpoints beyond those closest to us.

The messages you received as a child also taught you about yourself and others' expectations of you, building your personal belief system. These ideas and opinions come from those closest to us – parents, teachers, siblings and friends. The things they said and did and their way of relating to you and others laid the foundation for many of your beliefs, values and attitudes. Your parents' views, for obvious reasons, are particularly important. These beliefs tend to be centred around ideas of self-worth, achievement, acceptance and lovability.

Early messages have a lasting impact. It's as if they are set in concrete, solidly embedded in our brains, making them much harder to change. Just as we learn about the colour red or what a bird is, we also internalize the views held about us and these form our self-view and filter into the way we speak and relate to ourselves.

The transfer of information in childhood mostly takes place through everyday interactions. Children tune in to the subtle and not-so-subtle messages they are given, which influence how they think about themselves and the world around them.

While we generally and quite rightly trust our beliefs, like feelings they are not always right – it all depends on your experiences and what those closest to you said to you. If you were repeatedly told that you were clever, kind and capable, this is what you come to believe. But if you were negatively labelled or given confusing messages this can be problematic. When it comes to imposter syndrome certain experiences put you at higher risk.

Which experiences have an impact?

Children are wired to seek approval from their parents, so when it doesn't come this can lead to feelings of shame and humiliation. Without their parents' support or approval, or if they receive mixed messages, it's easy to conclude that their achievements are not important or impressive and they may learn to dismiss them as their parents do.

There are the obvious messages, such as being told you're not good enough, which can come in various forms: 'you're useless', 'this is typical of you', 'when will you ever learn?'. These negative messages can hurt all the more when they come from your parents – they see you every day, know you inside out and their opinion matters. As a child it's impossible to know that this is one person's view and that this person may not be a good judge, and so you internalize what they say as the truth.

If a parent only offers love or takes an interest when you are doing well or fitting in with them, and are conversely unhappy, cross or uninterested when you are not performing well, then this type of conditional love can also have a negative effect. Your parents' response to your schoolwork might be an indicator of this, for example when you bring home work and are told about all the ways you could improve it rather than earning approval. Or perhaps the things you do are never *quite* good enough.

Parents may also be uninterested. Lack of praise or positive feedback can be as problematic as negative feedback. When parents don't care about how you're doing and have little interest in you, or give a stock response to everything you do as brilliant with no differentiation, that affects children too. They aren't stupid; they know when they've put in the effort and when they haven't.

If you go on to be successful when you are older, this success collides with the old opinion you hold of yourself, making you believe that other people must be wrong about you and making you feel like an imposter.

One of the strongest predictors of imposter syndrome is having received mixed messages about achievement. For example, your test scores or teachers indicate one thing but your parents say something different – so you may achieve a top mark in your history exam, scoring 95 per cent, but your father asks why you didn't get 100 per cent.

Mixed or confusing messages from parents make it very difficult to internalize success as how you are doing is inconsistently reinforced. I once saw a client, Clemmie, who was extremely bright, but her mother believed that her achievements were not worthy of praise as they came so easily to her – she only rewarded her work when she did exceptionally well and never told her she was proud of her. Instead, she kept reminding Clemmie that doing well wasn't hard for her, so she shouldn't be too pleased about it. Yet her teachers were happy with her work and occasionally Clemmie overheard her mother boasting to friends about how brilliantly she was doing and what a genius she was. The two views just didn't add up.

Maybe there were two versions of what was going on in your life and the feeling of being a fraud was something you also felt when you were young. Your parents might have gone through a difficult divorce, putting your home life in turmoil, but at school no one knew about this and you carried on acting as if everything was OK.

Labels and comparisons

Families are prone to labelling different family members with particular characteristics, such as 'the disorganized one', 'the clever one', 'the rule-breaker'. These labels typecast the child and can become self-fulfilling. When you give a child a role this influences the others in the family: 'If he's the clever one, then I must be the stupid one.' Parents may also compare children negatively to others in the family such as a brighter sibling. Or the opposite can happen: you did well, but your parents were wary of singling you out for fear of the impact on another sibling, so your successes and achievements were never recognized, let alone celebrated.

Being labelled the clever one can also be a problem. Children who are taught that they are more intelligent than others or who have always found learning and new tasks easy, can develop imposter syndrome when they struggle to achieve something or become part of a peer group in which everyone is very clever. Many imposters secretly harbour the need to be the best compared with their peers. Often they have been top of the class through their school years, but in a larger setting such as university or the workplace they suddenly realize that there are lots of exceptional people and their own talents and abilities are not as special as they once thought. Not being the best can make them dismiss their own talents and see themselves as incompetent.

Subtle messages

Parents with the best of intentions might unintentionally build an unrealistic belief in their children: 'just do your best', can be turned inwardly into 'make sure it's perfect'. Or if your parents only rewarded effort then success that comes easily may feel undeserved.

Even a throwaway comment can have a lasting impact; you're not the cleverest, but you're a hard worker which may leave you feeling that you'll never have what it takes. Or someone else's reaction can have an effect, such as a best friend giving you the cold shoulder if they are put out by your success. You might conclude from this that you shouldn't take pleasure in doing well in case you upset others.

Family values that demand modesty, such as those of Dexter's family, can also have an effect.

While growing up Dexter was a talented flautist. He had natural flair and worked hard, with a dedication to practising and a quiet determination when it came to performances. Though nervous before competitions and recitals, he took them in his stride and frequently won at competitive events. His parents were always pleased with him, but never celebrated his achievements and they were rarely talked about, unlike those of his friends which were celebrated by their parents.

Dexter's father frowned on other parents talking about their children's successes. This was often discussed in a negative way and considered boastful: 'Did you hear Jenny going on about her kids again and how wonderful they are?' Dexter quickly learned that talking about your achievements wasn't a good thing and rarely shared how he was doing with others.

Dexter continued to do well, but each win felt less and less significant. He began to see his success as normal – expected rather than something to be proud of, leaving his measure of success distorted. No one made a big deal about it so he didn't either.

As an adult he set himself a much higher standard than others. He expected to be able to do everything flawlessly in every aspect of his life, with little recognition that he was doing well. He kept successes to himself and took little pleasure in his achievements, giving himself no opportunity to take on board how well he was doing.

Looking back at your history is not about blaming anyone, it's about understanding yourself better, questioning whether your beliefs are helping or hindering you and whether they are right. What we come to believe about ourselves – except for the more obvious negative messages – is not anyone's fault. In many cases, though by no means all, your parents were doing what they thought was right for you, based on their own experiences of being parented. Dexter's parents had probably also been brought up to believe that modesty was important, having inherited the belief from their parents.

If you weren't taught certain skills in childhood or given a healthy road map of how to behave, you can develop blind spots which you unwittingly pass on to the next generation. Parents are also human and are not immune to getting this wrong. Understanding this is another way to distance yourself from their view and acknowledge that it might not be correct.

Once you're aware of the different beliefs you hold, you then have a chance to question them and decide whether or not they are right for you now. I'll be showing you lots of different strategies to do this through the book, but for now I'd like you to simply reflect on what you've read so far in this chapter.

Reflect on the following:

- What messages did you receive as a child about your intelligence, ability, importance or value?
- Were there any significant events or experiences in your childhood that had an impact on you?
- What influence, if any, do you think these messages have had on you?

Your family's definition of success

We also build an idea of what success and failure look like and how to deal with them from our experiences within our family. Therefore the person you aspired to be like when you grew up will have an impact. Much of the learning that occurs through childhood is acquired through observation and imitation, and role models are very influential. They show you what can be achieved and provide guidance, motivation and inspiration. Most children's important role models are their parents and caregivers who have a regular presence in their lives. When you are a child, seeing your parents' lives informs your ideas of what you want from your life, either inspiring you or making you want to do something completely different, as well as acting as a model for how to handle things. If those closest to you treated mistakes or failure as unacceptable, then this is what you are likely to take on board.

They also inform your beliefs about competence. If you think back to Chapter 1 (page 40), your competence type was informed by your experiences growing up. If everyone told you how clever you were, you may have come to believe that if you're good at something you should find it easy (the Natural Genius), or that only perfection is good enough (the Perfectionist).

If your parents' definition of being bright was 'perfection with ease' then this skews your view. If you are unable to live up to this standard, you may jump to the conclusion that you're not doing well. Everyone around you sees you as academically able, but internally you believe that because it's not easy they can't be right about you and this can contribute to feelings of inadequacy.

If your family experiences conveyed the general message that intellectual ability, intelligence or competence is linked to how many degrees you hold then it's likely that you'll expect the same of yourself. Perhaps everyone in your family is a doctor, lawyer or accountant and you feel you must have a profession to be considered successful.

On the other hand, an absence of a role model or mentor can exacerbate imposter syndrome feelings, for example if you become the first in the family to attend college or have a career. These first-generation achievers can feel that they don't fit in anywhere – they are out of step at home and in their new environment.

When you have been given a clear message about what success means and you do something different – if for example your family considers having a profession to be a sign of success and you now work in the entertainment industry – this mismatch can make it very difficult to acknowledge your achievements.

You'll be more likely to question what you do and may believe that others take it less seriously. Even if you intuitively know you are successful it can be hard to feel this as you've been programmed to see success in the same terms as your family.

Take a moment to think all this through:

- How was success defined in your family?
- What was expected of you?
- Who were your role models?
- What was expected in terms of achievement?
- How did your parents react when you did well or when you struggled?

Think back to a time you were successful in your childhood and remember what happened.

- How were you treated?
- How did those closest to you respond to it and speak to you about it?
- What did your teachers say about it?
- What do you think the impact of this was on you?

Now think back to a time you made a mistake or failed in your childhood and ask yourself the same questions. Does what you do now match what was defined as success in your family?

As we grow older we become influenced by society and the groups we are part of – in our personal lives, at university, in our work. Those around us inform our beliefs and values, particularly if we look up to them, and this social conditioning continues to shape us, our self-concept and identity, as well as influencing our ideas of success and failure. If you are part of the corporate world and financial success is key this may become important to you. If arrogance is considered ugly and self-deprecation is important, you'll downplay your successes. If everyone works long hours, it won't seem strange if you do too.

Questioning old beliefs

Your personality, experiences and the definition of success in your family all combine to form your beliefs about yourself. People with imposter syndrome tend to conclude that they are not good enough, or that they are unworthy or inadequate in some way. They may not feel this all the time, but in situations where these feelings are triggered, and they feel unsure of what they are doing or unable to live up to other people's expectations, it feeds into the discomfort we looked at in Chapter 2 (page 51). Our beliefs have a big influence on our behaviours and we'll be looking at the different ways in which imposter syndrome can affect you in the next few chapters.

For now, I want to leave you with something to think about. You acquired these beliefs a long time ago and have been building on them ever since, but what if they weren't right in the first place? Based on your experiences it's completely understandable that you came to the conclusions you have. You built this view of the world based on the limited information you had access to growing up, but that doesn't mean it should remain unquestioned.

In fact, I'd say it's all the more important that you *do* question your beliefs, as they are so open to error. I'm sure you often re-evaluate most other important things in your life – your relationships, your progress towards a goal, or the things you want from your life – how we think about ourselves should be no different.

Our job over the course of this book is to break apart your view of yourself so you can look at it closely, re-evaluate it and put it back together in a new and better way. I want you to update your beliefs and work out what is important to you.

There are many different versions of success, whether it's a degree, practical achievements, being a stay-at-home parent, following an apprenticeship or working for a large company. What's most important is working out what success means to *you,* something we'll think about as you progress through the book. It can feel unsettling to dismantle everything, so think of this as a necessary step towards building solid foundations. It might feel strange, but it will make you feel more stable in the long term.

Chapter 4
Why don't we just update the belief?

'Our brains are not always rational – they become emotionally tangled with the ideas we believe to be true and resistant to ideas we think are false.'

By the end of this chapter you should:
- Understand how beliefs work
- Be able to recognize that your beliefs are not always correct
- Start to see how these beliefs affect you

You now have a good understanding of the beliefs you hold about yourself and where they came from. I hope it has also become clear that these beliefs are not always correct. Next I want to consider how the beliefs you hold affect you. We will be getting a little technical here! It is easy to assume that as you get older you naturally change your beliefs. While this sometimes happens, it's less likely to happen than you think, even when there's lots of evidence to disprove what you believe. You're a good example of this: you've had successes and been praised by others for your achievements. But rather than embrace this you still doubt yourself and your abilities. The reason for this? It's thanks to the core beliefs you still have about yourself. You can't update the belief – even though it might not be correct – because of the *impact* the belief has. I know this sounds a bit confusing, but stay with me and keep reading.

To make sense of this, we need to take a look at:

- The function of beliefs
- The impact of emotions on beliefs
- Confirmation bias
- Why you can't update your view of yourself

The function of beliefs

Our brains are constantly processing the information we receive through our senses. Beliefs are helpful as they lighten the cognitive load – they provide a framework to process information by referencing past experiences and memories when finding and interpreting new information.

Think back to the example in the last chapter (page 62): when you are repeatedly given a piece of information, such as what a bird is, you begin to identify them yourself and you can use this knowledge to identify other birds.

Similarly, our beliefs help us to make sense of the world around us by helping us to organize and interpret information. They allow us to take short cuts in interpreting the vast amount of information that is available in our environment.

If we tried to process everything as if we were encountering it for the first time, we wouldn't get much done. These short cuts allow us to follow routines without thinking too much about them and can filter our environment for what's relevant. Think of your morning routine or your route to work; it saves you time and energy to run some of your life on autopilot.

This means that, once formed, our beliefs are not just a view we hold, they also help us to interpret the outside world in terms of these existing expectations. They feed into everything we do and are central to how we operate in our lives. This is something we all do.

Beliefs help us to:

- Simplify the world – new information can be classified and categorized by comparing new experiences with existing beliefs
- Think quickly – we don't have to spend lots of time interpreting what's going on because our existing beliefs help us assimilate new information quickly and automatically
- Learn quickly – we learn more easily when information fits with our existing beliefs

This is a bit like using an online translation tool to work out how to say something in another language. If you had to look up every word individually it would take you a long time. Instead you can copy and paste words and phrases and find out in an instant how to say what you want to. The trouble is that the translation tool doesn't always get the meaning exactly right; it loses some of the subtleties of language and doesn't guarantee that you'll say words with the correct accent and intonation. It's helpful, but not completely reliable – a bit like our beliefs.

Importantly, our beliefs affect how we attend to information.

- They influence what we pay attention to – we're more likely to pay attention to ideas that fit with our beliefs
- They change how we treat information – when new information does not fit with existing beliefs, people sometimes distort or alter the new information to make it fit with what they already know
- They are very difficult to change – we often cling to our beliefs in the face of contradictory information

This bias is one of the reasons we hold on to our beliefs even when we are presented with a contradictory view. It has an impact on how we discover and interpret information, but if unchecked it can have some unfortunate side effects.

The impact of emotions on beliefs

We learn from those around us. But when we learn we don't simply take on board the messages we hear from those closest to us. An emotion goes with it too and our reasoning and emotions become fused into a belief. As a result, our brains are not always rational – they become emotionally entangled with the ideas we believe to be true and resistant to ideas we think are false. Think of the statement, 'I feel strongly about it.' There's a reason for the 'feel' part.

When you bring to mind a belief you recall not just the thought, but also the emotion attached to it. Thanks to evolution our emotions respond far more quickly than our rational reasoning – our highly responsive threat system reacts not just to predators, but to information too. The reasoning follows more slowly and deliberately, and by then our quick-fire emotions have already coloured our response (remember feelings aren't facts), skewing how we attend to information.

Beliefs that are set with strong emotions, such as a negative belief about yourself, are even more resistant to change. We hold them closely and they feel an inseparable part of us. This is why we can be so attached to negative beliefs even in the face of very reasonable evidence to the contrary. Once these beliefs are set we then gravitate to information that confirms our bias, cherry-picking the information that shows our view as correct. Gradually over the years we add more and more information in support of our view, even if the belief wasn't correct when it was formed. It's like having tunnel vision: you're focused only on information that proves your view right and are blinkered about everything else.

This process is called confirmation bias; the tendency to seek out and favour information that confirms our expectations and beliefs.

Confirmation bias

Leon Festinger, a renowned psychologist, wrote about a well-known example of confirmation bias in his book *A Theory of Cognitive Dissonance*. He infiltrated the Seekers, a small cult headed by Dorothy Martin, whose members thought they were communicating with aliens, one of whom they believed was the astral incarnation of Jesus Christ.

Dorothy transcribed interstellar messages through automatic writing. The group believed that on 21 December 1954 an apocalypse would occur, but that they would be rescued by the aliens. They left their jobs and partners and gave away their possessions to prepare for their departure.

When 21 December came and went, instead of doubting the prophecy and admitting that they had been wrong, the group found a new explanation – they had been spared at the last minute. Thanks to their willingness to believe in the prophecy they had managed to save Earth. They'd lost their jobs, their families and were mocked by the press, but still they maintained their belief. The fact that the apocalypse hadn't happened made them even *more* certain.

Confimation bias helps to explain the self-fulfilling nature of imposter syndrome. We pay more attention and place greater emphasis on evidence that supports our belief, while discrediting or ignoring any conflicting information. It means we interpret our experiences in ways that support our beliefs.

Confirmation bias not only influences how we interpret new information, it also helps to dictate what we look for in the first place and the memories we recall in response to certain questions and decisions. Confirmation bias is far more likely to occur when strong emotion is involved. If I don't want to believe that my partner is being unfaithful, or that my child is badly behaved, I can go to great lengths to explain away behaviour that seems obvious to everybody else – everybody who isn't too emotionally invested to accept it. Often this is automatic; we don't even notice we're doing it.

Think about something different from imposter syndrome that you feel completely sure about – such as your preferred political party or a favourite sports team. You do not hear or seek out any information against your view of them. The other political parties and their policies? They're rats! A rival sports team? Cheaters! Or recall a recent argument when you believed you were in the right. You can be so invested in being right that you ignore anything the other person says, building your own reasons and ignoring everything else. It's not until the level of emotion drops that you can start to hear what the other person is saying and consider their point of view.

See for yourself

Imposter syndrome is a perfect example of confirmation bias. You decided a long time ago that you were a fraud and for years you've been building an argument in support of this in your head, ignoring any information that doesn't fit and operating a strong bias against yourself. This unwavering belief is one of the biggest reasons you're unable to move forward. You're also scared of the potential shame and daren't risk a different approach, making it impossible for you to consider an alternative view.

You're certain you're right and that everyone else is wrong and will do everything in your power to prove it. You have different rules for when you do well and when you do badly, attributing success to external circumstances such as good fortune or luck, while if you do badly it's because of a personal failing. You've been doing this for so long now that it happens automatically. Good stuff? Reject. Negative information? You're all ears.

Constructive criticism, negative feedback and mistakes are all proof that you're not good enough. You go over them in your head and replay them in micro detail.

You never own your achievements and you'd certainly never celebrate them, keeping your focus on the reasons you don't deserve praise or credit. There's a long, long list of reasons for downplaying your successes – below are just a few you might recognize.

General:
- I got lucky or it was a fluke
- I'm a good actor
- I fooled them

- It's because they like me, they're being polite, or it's a social courtesy
- It was nothing
- It sounds more impressive than it is
- I had a lot of help
- I just worked really hard
- If I can do it anyone can
- I was in the right place at the right time
- They have low standards
- They've made a mistake
- They felt sorry for me
- It's positive discrimination
- No one else wanted to do it
- It's only a matter of time before I'm found out

Getting a job:
- I had connections
- I'm good in interviews
- I look good on paper
- There were very few applicants

Academic:
- It must have been a weak year
- I was on the reserve list, so they didn't really want me
- They mixed up the marks
- They let in the wrong person
- It's an administrative error
- I picked an unpopular course

If someone gives you positive feedback or compliments you, not only do you dismiss it, you often add another layer by telling them why they are wrong, putting yourself down in the process. You'll say: 'It looked better than it was; I actually mucked up in a few places.'

Even seeing a task completed isn't enough to change your view thanks to your competence type. You do feel an initial sense of relief and accomplishment, but the feeling is fleeting. You then deny that completing the task was related to your ability and reject positive messages about your personal contribution as these messages do not fit with your perception of success. You have an idea in your head of how well you should do, setting yourself incredibly high standards as a result of the distorted view you hold of what competence means.

If there is a discrepancy between your actual and your ideal standards of success – which there always is, as the standards you set are impossible for anyone to reach – then you disregard what others say as their belief doesn't match your view of how you've done. So instead of making you feel better, success reinforces the feeling of fraudulence. Despite doing well, you have not reached the high expectations you set yourself and your concept of ideal success.

This process resembles putting shapes into a children's shape sorter. Positive information has to come in exactly the right shape and be put in at the right angle to go through. At the same time negative information is collected in a huge bucket, so everything falls in. This means you are unable to take on board positive feedback or own your achievements. No matter what others say you doubt your ability and have a sense that you fooled others to get where you are.

This is not a display of false modesty. There might be times when you see you're doing well and are capable, but how often you see this will depend on the severity of your imposter syndrome. At the moment your view of yourself never changes as you're not allowing any new information to be taken on board. In fact, most of the time you're barely aware of it as you're so focused on what you're not doing and where you went wrong. If it doesn't fit with your beliefs and your ideas of competence, then there's little chance of you thinking you've done well. With the current beliefs you hold, you have little hope of changing.

It's no wonder it's so difficult for you to internalize success and accept praise as valid. Throw in the strong emotional response and it's even harder to see things differently. This prevents you from updating your view of yourself or any of the beliefs you developed in childhood. It also means there is a disconnect from your successes.

Connect with success

Think of the mental time you give to the good stuff. Now think of the time you give to the things you're unhappy about. I don't need to hear your answer to know that you spend *much*, much longer on the things you're unhappy about.

If you're not replaying the good stuff in your mind or talking about it to others, it has no chance of sticking. As a result, you remain disconnected from your achievements. Even though there is a huge amount of evidence that proves a different view, you are unable to relate to it as it's something you never think about or discuss. You can see it sometimes, but it's as though you're looking through a pane of frosted glass so what you see is not very clear and you can't quite bring it into focus, which means you can't internalize it.

When I talk about internalizing success, I mean taking on board success and holding on to it in your mind, so it becomes something you know about yourself. Praise and positive feedback are great in the moment, but we need to be able to internalize them so we build an inner measure of how we're doing.

External validation on its own is precarious as it's always reliant on someone or something else. However, an inner log is far more accurate and stable as it takes in everything you're doing and allows you to look back and see a fuller picture of your capabilities. You can draw on this when you feel unsure of yourself, which brings a sense of calm in knowing what you are capable of.

When you have no connection to what you have done this maintains the problem.

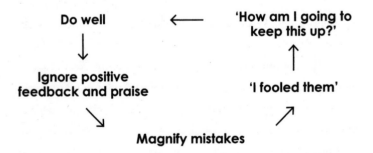

Even if you never make another mistake, do incredible work and win regular praise for the rest of your life, your view won't shift. It can't because you're not allowing any of this information in, so you are stuck in the time when the belief was set.

The good news is that you can fight against this confirmation bias. It takes hard work and you have to want to actively disprove it, but if you familiarize yourself with the different processes it will become easier to identify them and to make changes, so you can acknowledge your successes and see yourself as worthy. You need to take the emotion out of it and look at the evidence instead.

Review and re-evaluate

You now have a good understanding of what causes imposter syndrome and why the belief remains even though there's so much new evidence to counter it. Based on the biased information you see, your conclusions are right, but you're only seeing a very small part of the picture. I need you to take a few steps back, so you can take everything in and admire the view.

To do this, you need to put emotion to one side and look at the evidence instead. Write down all your successes by going through *everything* you have *ever* done, no matter how big or small. Take plenty of time to do this and to do it thoroughly. It will take a long time, but this will be time well spent. Don't worry, taking on board this new information doesn't mean you'll get too big for your boots. You have bigger boots to fill now and it's time you recognized that.

Think of this as gathering evidence against your imposter belief. Without this, you cannot update your confirmation bias and it will be much harder to actively pay attention to new information. Writing down everything you have done will allow you to take time to think about your achievements, take them all in and see them written down in black and white.

Explore every achievement you can think of – write anything down, no matter how big or small. If something comes into your head, note it down. Don't question it; don't allow any excuses to get in the way – for now just put them to one side. All I want to know is what's happened – not how or why.

Include the following:

- Exams and qualifications
- Job promotions and salary increases
- Compliments and praise from friends, family or colleagues
- Taking on roles such as chairing a meeting, running the PTA, becoming the lead or head of an area
- Difficult situations you've overcome, interviews, tough classes
- Personal successes in your family life or hobbies

Give your list the title 'My Achievements'. There are no right or wrong items to include; everything counts. You might want to do this over the course of a week or several days, as once you start to look back at your life, more ideas will gradually come to mind and you'll be able to add to this list.

Once you've completed it, read through what you've written down. See what you've accomplished? Imagine if I told you someone else had done all these things. What would you think of them as a person? What if someone else saw this list – what might they think of you?

This list gives you a very different picture from the one you hold in your head. You should be using this list to form your ideas of who you are and what you're capable of. Keep it in mind, hold it tight, make sure you reread this list every day and be ready to add to and build on this new belief.

Your negative bias has been keeping your problem going for far too long. It's clear that your belief that you are an imposter is not based on facts. It's caused by a feeling. I'm sure you're still discrediting it in part, but there's much more we can do to show you that this list is *you*. This list is what you're capable of, not trickery or luck; you're not such a good actor that you could have fooled everyone.

Next steps

It's time to be honest with yourself; as humans we're prone to bias. With this in mind I want you to stop for a moment and think through all you've covered.

Consider all your different reasons for believing the imposter view of yourself:

- Isn't it strange that you need so many different voices and tactics to convince yourself you're an imposter?
- Notice how the arguments and reasons change to suit whatever the success might be
- Can it be true that any success is external to you, while failures are entirely your doing?
- Do you apply the same rules to everyone else?

I hope it's becoming clearer that everything doesn't add up. To me the fact that there's no solid argument for your belief suggests that you're not right about yourself. If you suspect that the belief you hold about yourself isn't true, then hold on to this thought. To succeed in changing you need to loosen your long-held beliefs, starting by making a few cracks in them. Then when you hold them a little less tightly, you will have some room to consider this new view.

Chapter 5
The imposter twins: overworking and avoidance

'You've been doing your best, but rather than making things better, your coping strategies have made everything worse.'

By the end of this chapter you should:
- Recognize how your beliefs influence the coping strategies you use from day-to-day
- Start to consider the impact these coping strategies have on the way you interact with the world

You now have a good understanding of what imposter syndrome is and why it's affecting you, as well as an awareness of the beliefs you hold about yourself and why these keep you disconnected from your achievements. I want to complete the picture by showing you how these beliefs influence the coping strategies you use from day to day and by encouraging you to consider the impact of these strategies on how you tackle tasks and interact with the world.

These coping strategies manifest themselves in one of two ways, which I call the imposter twins – overworking and avoidance. They are another reason you remain disconnected from the good things you are doing, leaving your identity stuck in the past. Use this chapter as a checklist to understand how imposter syndrome is affecting you and the coping strategies you're using.

Problem coping strategies

When you live with the fear that you might be an imposter – no matter how deep down it lurks – you'll do anything to stay under the radar and to avoid the shame it makes you feel. As a result, you've put in place certain coping strategies over the years to manage your life, stay safe and prevent others finding out the truth.

We all use coping strategies to manage from day to day. They help us to master, tolerate, reduce or minimize stressful events. We also develop them in response to the beliefs we hold about ourselves. If I worry that I'm not good enough, then I'll develop a coping strategy to ensure that no one ever sees this and to keep this thought at bay. Often, these are coping skills we learned growing up, developed in response to the events we experienced.

Some coping strategies can be helpful – for example, learning that you feel better if you talk to someone, or doing exercise to de-stress and boost your mood. These are active coping strategies and are beneficial. Some strategies, however, add to the problem – such as cutting yourself off from your emotions or never telling others how you feel. These avoidant coping strategies prevent us addressing the problem.

If you think back to some of the experiences that can lead to feelings of imposter syndrome, it makes sense that you wanted to find a way to make yourself feel better. If you were the less clever sibling you might have vowed to always work hard and so overworked. Or if there were high expectations of you, you might have decided that you'd rather not try things you were unsure of, rather than try them and potentially fail; this is avoidance.

Based on your interpretation your response is understandable: if you really were a fraud then you'd need to do these things to ensure that you were not found out. Everything you do is aimed at preventing others finding out the 'truth' and to some extent your strategies work. In the short-term your coping strategies make you feel better, safer and mean that you won't be discovered. But if your beliefs about yourself are wrong and you are not an imposter, as I suspect, then these behaviours are part of the problem.

The old lady who swallowed a fly

This might sound strange, but these strategies make me think of the nursery rhyme about the old lady who swallowed a fly. She thought she might die as a result of swallowing the fly. If you're *that* scared, what happened next is not so ridiculous!

To remove the fly from her stomach, she swallows a spider to catch it, and then swallows a bird to catch the spider, a cat to catch the bird, a dog to catch the cat and so on, until she swallows a horse (and dies).

Fear can drive us to do things without really thinking them through – as you know all too well. When you're scared, you don't feel that you can even consider taking a risk, but what if the old lady had just ignored the fly and seen it as a bit of extra protein?

Just like the old lady, you might think that your coping strategies are helping, but in fact they are making everything worse and preventing you seeing the truth. The imposter thoughts and discomfort that you experience are like the fly; they're nothing to fear. You are more than capable of doing what you want to do, and even if you did make a mistake or fail, this wouldn't unmask you. Mistakes and failure are a normal part of life, not a death sentence.

You might feel that it's easier to keep going than to risk letting go and trying another way, but taking that risk is the only way to really see the truth. I hope that by now there are enough cracks in your imposter belief that you are starting to recognize that you might not be right about yourself. If the belief is wrong, then it makes sense to to re-evaluate your coping strategies too.

These coping strategies also prevent you changing your view of yourself . They keep the problem going and prevent you learning that you are not an imposter.

Your horse, cow, goat, dog, cat, bird and spider are:

- Secrecy
- Overworking and avoidance
- Self-criticism
- Self-doubt and insecurity
- Perfectionism and a fear of failure
- Unrealistically high standards
- Discounting positives and magnifying negatives

Let's take a look at the different ways overworking and avoidance can show themselves; some you'll be familiar with and some are subtler. As you read, make a note of those which apply to you and consider how they are having an impact on your life. If you step back and see the problems they cause this will help you find the confidence to make changes.

Overworking

The feeling that you are a fraud inspires greater effort and conscientiousness because you imagine that everyone else is more capable and intelligent than you. You believe you must work extra hard to cover this up.

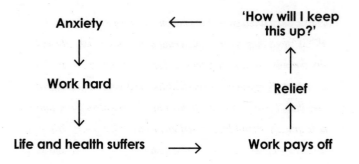

Overworking becomes problematic when the effort and energy you invest in a task exceeds that needed to produce work of a reasonable quality and interferes with other priorities such as relationships, hobbies or fun. Often you can see the problems that overworking is causing you, but feel unable to break the cycle for fear that this is what makes you good at your job. You worry that if you do not do well enough you might receive negative feedback or fail.

Overworking leads to:

- Working long hours and weekends
- Obsessing over minor details
- Over-preparing
- Overstudying
- Reading and rereading emails
- Excessive attention to detail
- Self-criticism
- Self-doubt
- Perfectionism
- Trying to stay in control at all times
- Impossibly high standards
- Moving goalposts

William had been given a promotion. A reorganization at work had resulted in several people being made redundant. He had survived the cuts and had not only been promoted, but was also given two other people's responsibilities. His boss had convinced him that this was a credit to his ability, reassuring him that he'd quickly streamline the different roles into one. William felt excited about the prospect of a more senior and visible role in the company.

When he started the new job he was unbelievably busy. William was so pleased that he'd been given this opportunity; he didn't want to make a big deal of any aspect of it, feeling sure that if he just worked hard enough he could get everything under control. When the work kept piling up, he concluded that he wasn't effective enough yet, rather than seeing the quantity of work as the problem. He felt sure that his colleagues would be able to handle it if they were given the same chance. So he kept quiet, not wanting to look as though he wasn't coping, believing that if his performance slipped he'd be kicked out of the company and a queue of replacements would be waiting to take over where he had left off.

Instead he left the office later and later. He never met up with friends as he couldn't leave early enough or manage the workload the next day if he'd had a drink. On the days when he picked up his children, he'd put them to bed and then turn his laptop back on. When friends showed concern for him, he quickly shut them down, explaining that it was temporary and not too bad, telling himself that they didn't understand what it was like to be in a job like this.

Since beginning the new role William's eczema had flared up, but rather than recognize that this might be in response to the stress, he felt annoyed that he had another thing to deal with. At the weekends, he'd either work or sleep. He was exhausted by the

quantity of work he had to keep up with, but still he kept going.
William could only keep up by sacrificing his personal life, but he
didn't dare question this as he was worried he'd fall behind and
that his bosses would see he wasn't up to the job and feel they'd
misplaced their trust in him.

William's bosses were pleased with his work; after all he was handling three people's jobs. In their eyes, he was extremely efficient with excellent attention to detail. What boss wouldn't want an employee like that? Many companies rely on their employees overworking and purposely employ those who are more perfectionist, deliberately encouraging competition between employees and making them aware that they are lucky to have their job to further fuel anxiety and insecurity among employees, so they work even harder.

When you think about the competition for places in certain industries it's no wonder their employees feel insecure – in the five Magic Circle law firms (an elite group generally regarded as the five leading UK-headquartered law firms) there are 1,500 applicants for 90 places and of those, only 5 per cent make partner. When you're a lawyer you inhabit a highly competitive world. There are many others aspiring to do the job you do, so if you don't do it there are plenty of others who will.

This creates an ideal environment to promote insecurity and overworking as colleagues are pitched into competition with each other. You are rated against your peers and there is no transparency, so you're never quite sure how anyone else is doing. You know that everyone else is bright and capable to be working at a firm like this, so you set yourself incredibly high standards to keep up and these just get higher and higher.

You might have noticed that in some industries there are very few older people and there's a reason for this; they can't keep up this pace indefinitely or they'd burn out from overwork. Many companies do not have your best interests in mind but the best interests of the company. It's worth remembering where company loyalties lie when you're working yet another weekend.

Why doesn't success end the cycle?

Amazingly most imposters do meet their goals and succeed at whatever they put their mind to doing. Overworking means that you do get better at your job. You learn more, and this leads to more success and promotion just as William discovered, but rather than alleviating the underlying anxiety that you can't cope, you misattribute your success to hard work. Or if you do reach your goal, you shift the goalposts just a bit further out of reach, which serves to trigger more imposter feelings. This prevents you seeing that you've done well because *you* have done a good job and so you remain trapped in the overwork cycle.

Perhaps you're self-employed and doing well, but wonder how long this can last. Or you may be doing well in your field, but the better known you become the worse you feel. Increased visibility means that there are more eyes on you and you fear that others will be more likely to discover that you don't actually know what you're doing. As your success grows the scope for negative judgements or comments increases too.

Success or promotion, rather than silencing your fears or disproving your imposter theory, can feel crushing or terrifying. The change can mean that the standard you work to has been raised, either by you or by others. Expectations increase and there is more at stake; you now have a reputation to maintain and the responsibility feels a burden. Rather than basking in your achievements you wait in dread, imagining how everyone will laugh when they find out the truth.

Your anxiety increases and this adds to your fears that if something goes wrong, everything else will unravel: 'What happens if it all falls away?' The higher you climb, the more insecure you feel as you have further to fall and the pressure grows. You feel that your career is a disaster waiting to happen and you are convinced that this time everything will be uncovered.

The insecurity that drives you does make you more conscientious and helps you to succeed. The secondary gain from this makes it hard to let go of – doing well gives you a thrill, and there is a part of you that likes the fact you're working hard and doing more than other people. However, you don't take on board your success thanks to your ever rising standards and moving goalposts.

More importantly the success comes at a cost to your health, your relationships and your happiness, as you struggle to keep up with everything and are never happy with what you do. The amount of work you're doing makes it very difficult to enjoy the rest of your life and no matter how much you do, it never seems enough.

In fact you don't need to be working this hard; you're doing more than is necessary. I know this is hard to believe when you're the sort of person who feels they could always do more, but at the moment the premium is too high – it's like overpaying your insurance – and means you never give yourself the chance to see how well you are doing. The cycle needs to change.

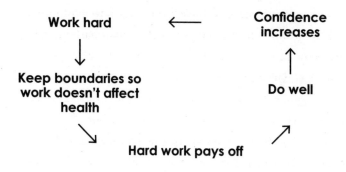

The reality is that no one does well without hard work and when you explain away your success, you're not recognizing your strengths. Working hard is a skill requiring perseverance, determination, concentration and the ability to acquire knowledge and learn. This does not come easily to most people: an important reminder for the Natural Geniuses among you.

Think about your life now and look closely at this overwork cycle; is this really how you wish to continue?

A simple way to think about it is to ask yourself: 'If I was at the end of my life looking back, what would I want to see? Would I have done anything differently? Who would I want to have spent my time with? What would my biggest regrets be?'

This is a powerful tool for seeing the bigger picture and gives you the opportunity to think about what's important to you. Not many people (especially people like you) reach the end of their lives thinking they wished they'd worked harder. Bronnie Ware is an Australian nurse who spent several years giving palliative care to patients during the last 12 weeks of their lives. She collected her observations in a book called *The Top Five Regrets of the Dying* and writes about the phenomenal clarity of vision that people gain at the end of their lives and how we might learn from this.

When questioned about regrets or anything they wished they'd done differently, the patients' responses centred around five common themes:

1. I wish I'd had the courage to live a life true to myself, not the life others expected of me
2. I wish I hadn't worked so hard
3. I wish I'd had the courage to express my feelings
4. I wish I had stayed in touch with my friends
5. I wish I had let myself be happier

These themes are all relevant to the way you're living at the moment, so take a minute to think about this and about what you want from your life.

Avoidance

When you aspire to such high standards and have an overwhelming fear of failure, it's no wonder that sometimes you avoid doing what you need to do, procrastinating when you just can't face the effort that starting involves or stopping halfway through when finishing seems too difficult.

Perhaps you wait until the last minute and find yourself in a situation that means you can't do a good job, so you pull an all-nighter, or have no time to check your work. Then at least you have a reason for not doing well; you can say to yourself, 'If I'd put the time in it would have been fine.'

You'd rather sabotage your chances than work really hard to do badly. In a warped way, this keeps all the balls in the air and you can maintain the belief that you could have been brilliant if you'd tried. The alternative fear is that if you'd tried and everything hadn't worked out everyone would judge you. This can also be a way of avoiding potential criticism or negative feedback.

Even if you succeed with this last-minute approach, you find it difficult to take on board the result – you didn't even try your best and still did well! You therefore discredit the exam or interview, telling yourself that it couldn't have been very hard, or the exam board or interviewer must have made a mistake.

Avoidance can also make an appearance in more subtle ways, such as not making a phone call to tackle a problem and then worrying that the other person will be annoyed, so putting it off for longer. This effort to control everything that happens in your life is an attempt to avoid feeling vulnerable. So you avoid situations that might reveal a weakness, or drink too many glasses of wine every evening to silence the worries.

Here are some common examples of avoidance:

- Avoiding difficult situations
- Struggling to be assertive
- Failing to ask for help
- Holding back
- Procrastinating
- Blaming others for making you feel inadequate
- Criticizing others for doing things wrong
- Under preparing
- Not using the phone

- Turning up late
- Undermining success
- Never taking risks
- Staying under the radar
- Not putting yourself forward for promotion
- Dreaming of escape – selling up and travelling or doing menial work

When avoidance becomes more serious it can lead to self-sabotage; you are driven by feelings of inadequacy and make it seem to others that you have an attitude problem, rather than recognizing your fears.

The following scenarios may occur:
- Not doing the work
- Not trying – a preference for not trying rather than failing
- Not caring – if you don't care it doesn't matter what happens
- Having a big night out before an important meeting
- Becoming socially withdrawn
- Applying for jobs which are beneath you
- Missing job opportunities
- Letting others down
- Substance misuse
- Self-destructive behaviours
- Never staying in one place for long – changing jobs, moving cities or countries

Research suggests that these avoidant coping strategies are a psychological risk factor or marker for adverse responses to stressful life events. They are like burying your head in the sand; you might hide away for a while, but everything will still be there and unchanged when you come up for air.

> *Cara had decided that she was ready to go back to work. She arranged to go to a networking event; she felt nervous at the prospect of putting herself out there. Before going she prepared how she'd approach it, telling herself that this was a starting point and it didn't matter what came of it, she should just go along. When the day came she did her best to chat, tell people about herself and find out about them. The event went brilliantly, she met lots of interesting people, everyone responded really well to her and one of the key women there asked her to email her CV after the event. Cara couldn't believe how well it had gone and how much everyone had liked her.*
>
> *When she got home she vowed to email the woman the next day. The next day came and the next, but she couldn't quite get round to sitting down and thinking about it. She knew she had to get the wording just right before sending it; this was her big chance. Before she knew it, a week had passed. Finally, she forced herself to do it and immediately had a response – 'Thank you Cara, we'd love to meet you. Come in next week.'*

It can be helpful to become aware of the avoidant strategies you use and to understand why you use them. Fear of failure is a big part of the problem; you can feel very vulnerable when you go for something you really care about. You're putting yourself out there and it's understandable if, like Cara, you worry that it might not work out. But you'll have no chance if you don't try.

We'll look at strategies to manage the imposter twins later in the book, but for now, it's important to see how they operate and to update your conclusions. Instead of concluding that you did well through luck, recognize that you are good at working under pressure. Instead of seeing feedback as negative, see that it is useful and recognize that the more you hear other views, the more you'll become used to them. It can also help to realize that no one is watching you as closely as you imagine. They won't be shocked or look down on you if your worst-case scenario comes true and things don't work out. They're more preoccupied with their own lives; the scrutiny you put yourself under is far tougher than their opinions. And your worst-case scenario is just that: the *worst-case* scenario. It's unlikely to happen. As you've already discovered, things do work out, even when you don't put in your full effort. Imagine what you might be capable of if you let go of your fears and invested fully in what you want.

Moving forward

When I think about all this and the impact it's been having on you, I feel a great sadness. You've been doing your best, but rather than making things better your coping strategies have made everything worse. You came to the wrong conclusion about yourself a long time ago, but there is nothing wrong with you; with these strategies working against you you've never had a chance to find that out.

You've ended up building a prison around yourself which isolates you from those around you, so you never see your successes and swing between overworking and avoidance. What you thought was keeping you safe and protecting you is actually a trap. You don't need to continue to do all these things.

Before you move on, I want you to consider everything in this chapter and think about what you want for yourself.

- How have your coping strategies been affecting you?
- Are you sacrificing your health and happiness for your work or your relationships?
- What would it be like to have some boundaries so there was space for you?
- How might it feel to really go for the things you want?
- If these coping strategies are not working, what could you do instead?
- Who do you know who has a good approach to work or their relationships? How do they make this work?

In the next part of the book, I'll help you to explore these questions. The answers aren't straightforward, but it is helpful to start entertaining a new approach. And in the third part I'll encourage you to drop the coping strategies that aren't working and build new ones that do work. It's time for you to take ownership of what's happening in your life. The next step is a big one, but it's the only way you will be able to see for sure that the reason you are doing well is not thanks to these coping strategies, but in spite of them.

PART II

WHY YOU ARE NOT
AN IMPOSTER

Chapter 6
Testing out the theory

**'You need to let go of imposter
syndrome to move forward.
Say goodbye to it, wave it off
into the sunset.'**

By the end of this chapter you should:
- Recognize that your theory that you are an imposter does not stand up under scrutiny
- Have begun the process of letting go of imposter syndrome by deciding to change, and by choosing to alter your view of yourself

There are now a few cracks appearing in your imposter beliefs, but I'm sure you still have a lot further to go. This next part of the book will help you begin to change. One by one we will look at the internal thought patterns and beliefs that support imposter syndrome and I will show you what's wrong with them and why they need to be changed. And in the third part of the book we will implement practices for change.

Let's think about this as two theories. *Your* theory is that you are an imposter. You need to do everything in your power to hide it and avoid being found out. When you live with the fear that you might be an imposter – no matter how deep it lurks – you'll do anything to stay under the radar and to avoid the shame it makes you feel. As a result, you've put certain coping strategies in place to manage your life, stay safe and prevent others knowing the truth.

This means you are keeping your fears a secret, working extra hard, avoiding speaking up, not owning achievements, dwelling on mistakes and never going for things for fear that you're not good enough. If you're right, these elaborate strategies ensure that people never find out the truth. But if your beliefs are wrong and you are not an imposter, as I suspect, then these behaviours are part of the problem.

My theory is that you worry you're an imposter and that the strategies you're using prevent you from seeing the truth. If my theory is right and this is a worry problem, then you need to be doing the opposite of what you are doing. At the moment, you're digging to get out of a hole – you might feel this is helping, but it's making everything worse. You need to stop using these coping strategies, start taking risks, talk about your fears and let go of the punishing standards that prevent you from seeing how well you're doing. Only if you stop will you see that you are acting on an emotion rather than a fact.

My theory is based on psychological research and the clinical experience I've gained from working with many people who suffer with this problem. Your theory is based on a feeling that you're not as good as you're pretending to be.

You believe you're the only one, but you forget that you only know what's going on inside your own head. You only hear your own fears and worries. You compare how you feel inside with what you see of other people's outsides, imagining they don't have the same insecurities or fears. In consequence you judge yourself as lacking. It can be all too easy to forget that others feel this too.

My job puts me in an incredibly privileged position. I work with some amazing people and they give me an insight into their world. They tell me their darkest secrets and their greatest fears, their insecurities and sadness. This means that I *know* we are all similar under the surface. No one is on top of everything (including me) and there is so much overlap in people's insecurities and fears. Rather than making us different, this is part of what makes us human. I want you to see this too and realize that you are more than good enough exactly as you are. That's why it's so important we disprove your theory.

I've summarized the two theories below, so you can see them side by side. Take some time to consider everything in the table. This can't go on!

YOUR THEORY	MY THEORY
I am an imposter.	You worry you're an imposter.
I'm not good enough (an underlying sense of this, or a feeling you have all the time).	You came to this conclusion as a result of your experiences and thanks to your confirmation bias it's difficult to see a different view.
I must keep my fears a secret.	Keeping your beliefs secret prevents you finding out that you are not alone and recognizing that this is a common problem.
I'm not up to the task.	Insecurity is an understandable human response to the discomfort you feel before trying something new. But feelings are not facts – this discomfort doesn't mean you are an imposter or that you can't make a go of things.
I must never fail or I'll be found out.	Failure is a normal part of life; it helps you learn and increases resilience.
I need to do everything perfectly. I must set myself incredibly high standards to avoid being found out.	Striving for perfection and the rules you set yourself add to your feeling of inadequacy – your standards are incredibly difficult to reach, so you constantly feel you are falling short.
I have to work harder than everyone else to avoid detection.	The effort and energy invested is more than necessary and interferes with priorities such as friends and hobbies. You never have a chance to see this as you daren't do less.
I never listen to or believe positive feedback if it doesn't match up with what I expect of myself.	This means you never take on board any information that shows you are doing well, making it impossible to update your view of yourself.
I credit my achievements to luck, contacts, charm or timing.	Everyone gains benefits from these things, but they account for a tiny percentage of your success.

YOUR THEORY	MY THEORY
I need to be self-critical if I want to reach my goals and keep myself in check.	Your self-critical commentary is demotivating and leaves you feeling even worse about yourself.
I focus solely on mistakes and ways I can improve and see these as confirmation that I am an imposter.	Everyone makes mistakes. They are not proof that you are an imposter, but a sign of being human.
I avoid things when everything gets too much.	Avoidance makes you feel even worse and means you don't give yourself a proper chance.
I never put myself forward; I make sure I don't stand out.	You don't give yourself a chance to see that you could have done well.
Everyone else is capable and knows what they're doing.	Everyone shares the same insecurities and fears.
I'm right about myself and everyone else is wrong.	This makes it impossible to update your identity and consider an alternative view.

What is the evidence?

This theory you've been holding tightly to is based on a sample of one (you) rather than actual evidence.

If this was psychological research it wouldn't be published. The evidence you're using at the moment is not based on fact and doesn't stand up to scrutiny. If your coping strategies did work, I'd have been taught them when I was training, but at no point on the doctorate course did anyone endorse self-criticism, perfectionism, overworking or avoidance. Rather these were seen as problems to overcome.

Over the next few chapters I'm going to help you to build a dossier of evidence for my theory. This will be based on facts, rather than thoughts and feelings, so you can let go of the belief that you're an imposter and the strategies that are holding you back. We will then look at effective strategies you can use to keep imposter syndrome at bay and live the life you deserve.

Remember to keep track of all the evidence and make a note of times when you see you're doing well or that you are capable. Hold on to them – these thoughts are often fleeting; try to focus on them for as long as you can and give them the time they deserve. These are the cracks in your theory. We want to widen the cracks and let in more light so you can see that the old belief is just not right.

Changing the pathway

I want you to think about your current belief as a well-worn path. When you're in a situation that triggers these beliefs, your brain heads straight down the path that tells you you're an imposter, not good enough or have achieved something thanks to external circumstances. The path is so well worn that you can practically slide down it, sinking into a revolting swamp at the bottom that makes you feel even worse.

There was a time when you didn't even realize that this was happening. You were unaware of the impact of your coping strategies and thinking patterns and how they maintain the problem. When reactions are automatic, it's understandable that you slide every time into the swamp. This isn't your fault. But now you are aware of what's happening, you have a responsibility to yourself to change and recognize this belief for what it is – a lie – and take action. This will prevent an automatic reaction and offer you a moment of choice.

Changing your belief about yourself means finding a new path. At the moment that path is overgrown and difficult to follow. There are signs to a new pathway and you do sometimes take this route when you're feeling good about yourself. But it's harder to get down; there are thorny bushes on either side that scratch you and there are patches of stinging nettles to dodge as you go. You have to pay attention to work out the way through, but once you reach the end you're in a much nicer place. The view is beautiful; it's calmer and you feel much better when you're there.

You should already have started to notice imposter thoughts. Also notice the discomfort when they recur. Hear the arguments against yourself and recognize the competence type you fall into. Doing this is an excellent start and an example of a point at which you can make a choice: a 'choice point'. A choice point gives you the opportunity to step back and ask yourself which path you want to take. Do you want to go along with the imposter voice or take a different route to a better, calmer place?

The new path will be difficult to navigate at first; you'll have to switch out of autopilot and remember the way. The more often you go down the new path, the easier it will become, as you tread down the stinging nettles and cut back the brambles. Your old belief will be the same and it will be hard to challenge at first, but challenging it will soon become second nature and the end result will be worth the effort.

You won't always succeed, but every time you do you're wearing down that new route. The rest of the book will teach you strategies to help you take the path to the great uplifting view and not the swamp. They play the part of your lawnmower, gardening gloves and hedge cutters, making the path easier to navigate. We'll also add to what you see – binoculars, flowers, a cool breeze and sunshine.

Let go of imposter syndrome

Before you can take this new path, you have to decide that you *want* to walk down it. Strange as this may sound, letting go can feel like a loss. Imposter syndrome is what you've always known. It feels familiar and has been with you so long that it gives you a sense of security. Making a change can be daunting. Some people are reluctant to admit being wrong, as this would mean they'd suffered without needing to and have potentially missed out on a lot.

For many people imposter syndrome seems to bring some advantages: it makes you work harder, aim higher, do better. It keeps you on your toes, stops you getting big-headed or complacent and tells you that you shouldn't get used to doing well in case it all falls away.

Over the years, the imposter voice has convinced you that you're the problem and that it is keeping you safe – that its control over you is caring and you can't go it alone. Your self-esteem has become so low that you believe this. You daren't do things differently as the risk feels too great. I'm sorry to break it to you, but if this was a relationship it would be an abusive one. You don't need to treat yourself in this way to do well. This voice is not what's keeping you on your toes and working hard. You are the one who is doing this; it's the person you are.

Take a moment to think about *why* you are holding on to it – maybe you're keeping yourself small so you can always be right, or it's a way to ensure you become the very best. The reasons are slightly different for everyone, but finding your reason will help you to step away from it.

You need to let go of imposter syndrome to move forward. Say goodbye to it, wave it off into the sunset or write it on a piece of paper then rip up the paper and throw it away – whatever works for you.

Choose to change your view

When you're working on changing your belief, it can be helpful to think of the belief operating in the same way as a prejudice. Can you think of someone in your life who has a prejudice against a group of people that you can see is wrong?

Perhaps your friend is a man who believes that women are inferior to men. When he sees a woman and she is not doing as well as a man at a task, what does he say? I'm guessing he'll point out that it reinforces his point.

Now, what might he say when he sees a woman doing something as well as or better than a man? Maybe he'll say it's a fluke, or that the woman must have cheated, or that she's the exception to the rule. Perhaps he even ignores her and claims he hasn't seen her. One observation is not going to convince him to change his view.

What if you wanted to change his view; how would you go about it? First, he'd have to want to change it, then you'd need to show him lots of examples of contradictory information. You'd also need him to keep track of it, so he can't deny it or quickly forget it as his belief will push him to do.

The beliefs you hold about yourself act just like this prejudice. No matter how much new information contradicts your beliefs, you're reluctant to change your view. As with a prejudice, you discount any positive feedback and distort the reality of what's going on to suit your view. When it's impossible to refute your claim, you believe it's a one-off and if all else fails you just ignore it.

Changing your view is not straightforward. You have so many ways to cling on to it. To give you a better chance of seeing and hearing the new information, I want you to use the following strategies as you work through the rest of the book.

Externalize the imposter voice

The first strategy is to externalize the imposter voice. This might sound a bit strange! You need to see that this is not *your* voice, but the voice of your fears. The better you get at spotting the imposter voice in action, the more successfully the strategies will work.

Think of this voice as a bully. Every day it tells you that you're not good enough, you need to work harder, never fail and do everything perfectly – and threatens that if you don't everyone will know you're a fraud. The voice scares you into doing what it wants, promising to keep you safe, but this voice is your enemy not your friend. It doesn't have your best interests in mind.

If the idea of a bully doesn't work for you, you can turn the voice into another person, a creature or someone ridiculous that you can laugh at – anything that helps you to disown it and see that this voice is not worth listening to. One client called his voice

Gobby and imagined it as an ugly little goblin. Every time he felt the imposter voice creeping in, he would say out loud, 'Go away Gobby.' Sometimes he was a little ruder than that! It was transformative for him.

Thoughts aren't facts

Now you recognize the voice as the imposter voice, one key idea to hold on to is that if the voice tells you that something is true, that doesn't mean it is true. You may feel like an imposter, but that doesn't mean you are one. Of course your thoughts and feelings are useful, but they only form part of the picture, especially when it comes to anything imposter syndrome related.

When you hear the voice, remind yourself that the imposter voice is a thought, not a fact. There's always more than one perspective. When you feel discomfort remind yourself that this is just how you feel, not how things are. When these thoughts and feelings come up think about the different possible explanations there might be.

Ask yourself:

- What's the evidence for this?
- Would it stand up in a court of law?
- What else could be going on here?
- How would I see this if a friend was telling me about it?
- Do I have any experiences that show a different view?

If you're unable to challenge it, simply recognize it as the imposter voice; don't give it importance or believe it is correct. I'll help you to do this using different strategies, but for now, this is a good starting point.

Talk to other people

You've been actively building your view that only you feel like this, ignoring any evidence that this affects others too. To really believe that how you feel is no different from the way other people feel you have to start talking more openly about what's going on. This is the only way for you to be sure that when others look confident and capable they may not feel that way all the time.

Since I started writing this book I have been looking for examples of people who suffer from the doubts that come with imposter syndrome. And I have found so many, from actors and writers to singers, sports stars and entrepreneurs — so you're one of an all-star cast!

Start looking out for others who experience these feelings. Find ways to bring up the topic in conversation and talk about your experiences and anxieties, admit mistakes and show vulnerability. If you can, find humour in it; laughing can take the power out of it and leave you feeling lighter. This will make you closer to others, help them to understand you better and will allow them to feel comfortable opening up to you in return.

You can't control everything

Finally, as you work through the strategies I want you to keep in mind that you can't be completely responsible for how life goes. This idea might sound a little worrying, but bear with me. At the moment you see yourself as completely responsible for making everything go well. The converse of this is that you also take responsibility for anything that goes wrong. When it goes wrong you blame yourself – you should have prevented it, seen it would happen, tried harder – obsessing, planning and always trying to stay in control. Trying to make everything go well all the time requires a lot of work and a great deal of energy.

You're taking too much responsibility for making things go well, forgetting about the other people involved and their shared responsibility. You're also forgetting that life doesn't always run smoothly. No matter how hard you try, there's no route through life that is pain-free and in trying to prevent anything ever going wrong you're causing yourself much greater stress. Things do sometimes go wrong, but you will get over it and see that often the outcome is even better.

You're also missing a chance to see that even without superhuman effort at all times, things are generally OK and they do work out well. This is a bit like spinning plates: you don't need to hold the poles all the time, you can stand back and watch them spin. Trusting in this is like releasing a heavy weight, setting you free from the burden you have been carrying. You don't need to force everything or put yourself under this immense pressure.

Letting go doesn't mean that everything will always work out well, but that's OK. Much as we like to believe it, we are not the masters of our own destiny. Stop for a minute and think about this. What if you aren't in complete control of everything? What if you've been trying to stay on top of everything and in charge when everything would have been fine without you? This idea is something I want you to get used to!

Hold on to these key ideas:

- Choose to change your view – wave goodbye to imposter syndrome
- There are two theories; yours versus mine
- What's the evidence? Would it stand up in a law court?
- Which path do you wish to take? Find the choice point
- Externalize the imposter voice
- Thoughts and feelings aren't facts
- Talk to other people
- You can't control everything

Chapter 7
Compassion:
the antidote to
self-criticism

'Think of compassion as the
mortar that holds everything
together, so you can confidently
rebuild the bricks of who you are
and how you operate.'

By the end of this chapter you should:
- See that compassion is far better than self-criticism
- Understand the value of reflection

In the next part of the book I'll dismantle the theory that you are an imposter. I will then prove that you only *think* you are one. To do this I'll look at each of your arguments in turn. I'll also introduce lots of strategies to enable you to build your belief in yourself and see your theory for what it is: a lie.

The first argument I want to examine is the idea that self-criticism is beneficial and something you require to succeed. If you continue with the level of self-criticism you have been used to, you won't get far with the strategies I'm introducing. All the research shows that self-criticism makes you *less* effective at implementing coping strategies. It's for this reason that I am introducing self-compassion.

Compassion is key to overcoming imposter syndrome and it needs to be at the core of every strategy you undertake. Think of it as the mortar that holds everything together, so you can confidently rebuild the bricks of who you are and how you operate. This will leave you feeling much stronger and when you try the new strategies they are more likely to be effective.

Before you can think about a new way of speaking to yourself, you first need to see the problems with your current approach. This is a two-step process. Step one is to tune in to your internal commentary and step two is to find a new more compassionate voice.

Self-criticism

Look back at the last chapter and the theories table and think about what it means to feel an imposter. It's clear that it allows no room for being nice to yourself. The fear of failure, self-doubt, the sense of not being good enough and aiming for impossible standards all result in a daily stream of self-criticism.

Everyone has self-critical thoughts from time to time – it depends on the day, your mood and what's going on in your life. But when you get them it's important to see them for what they are: a hindrance rather than a help.

Self-criticism preys on what's most important to you and makes everything seem worse than it is. This is bad enough when things are going well, but when you make a mistake or fail, you will experience an onslaught of abuse.

Here are some of the things you tend to do:

- See things as black and white rather than in shades of grey
- Ruminate repeatedly over your mistakes
- Fear failure intensely
- Always feel that you could have done more
- Self-scrutinize and overanalyse
- Imagine that others are judging or thinking negatively about you

Why are we so busy being mean to ourselves? When you think back to your experiences, there's a good chance that you were never taught how to be compassionate to yourself. How can you know how to do something if you've never been shown?

Just as we learn words from our parents to communicate with others, the way we are spoken to also helps us to develop the language we use internally. If you had a critical parent, were negatively compared to others or received mixed messages about how you were doing then it's likely that you have internalized these ways of relating to yourself. Without praise, it's difficult to develop self-belief or to learn the language necessary for positive self-motivation, encouragement, reassurance and the ability to take on board your achievements.

Some people may have come to believe that they need self-criticism to ensure that they don't slack. Over the years they have learned to motivate themselves in this way. There's a widely held belief that you need to be self-critical if you want to work hard or do well, that you have to suffer to succeed and that without self-criticism you might become complacent or put in less effort.

In my work as a psychologist, I've yet to find any evidence that backs this up. In fact, I'd go so far as to say that constantly criticizing yourself has the opposite effect. This negative internal monologue doesn't just make you feel bad about yourself, it can also make it harder to achieve your goals.

Self-criticism puts you at higher risk of depression and stress and it makes you less effective at implementing coping strategies. Rather than motivating you, it paves the way for anxiety and low self-esteem. Put simply, if you speak in a horrible way to yourself all the time you're going to make yourself feel bad.

By comparison, self-compassionate people are more resilient and bounce back more easily from setbacks. They are more likely to learn from their mistakes, to take steps to improve themselves and to reach their potential.

Try to recall a time when you faced a really difficult challenge, whether it was a goal you wanted to reach, a big work project or a relationship break-up. Who helped you through? I'm guessing it wasn't someone who shouted at you and told you how useless you were. Think about your role as a friend or parent: would you use criticism to help and support someone you care about? Of course not. If things are difficult you need support, not telling off.

The trouble is that self-critical ideas are some of the hardest to shift. Because of the way our brains have evolved we register negative thoughts more quickly than positive ones and are programmed to focus on the negative.

Alf had gone to university and realized it wasn't for him, so he dropped out and went to work in an office. He enjoyed it, but the culture didn't suit him and so he handed in his notice and took some time to really consider what he wanted to do. After serious deliberation he decided to go into TV and managed to get a job as a runner. He knew that he had to make this job work; after two failures he felt this was his last chance.

The TV work culture meant working long hours and earning little praise. When his bosses occasionally gave Alf good feedback, he hardly heard the words because he was so focused on improving. He didn't want to get complacent, so he concentrated instead on his mistakes and what he needed to do to improve. When he did occasionally forget items for a shoot or miss a deadline he would focus exclusively on these mistakes, making himself feel even worse.

Alf worked hard and his hard work paid off – a year into the job he was marked out as one to watch. Although part of him was surprised, deep down he did believe in himself – more than that, he believed that if he kept going he could be one of the best, but this put him under more pressure. Although at times he could see how well he was doing, in his head he was still the boy who had failed twice.

When he moved on to a new project with a critical boss, the combination of his inner voice and his boss resulted in Alf being signed off work with anxiety. It was then that he came to see me. We worked on developing a more compassionate inner voice and

Alf soon learned to back himself and recognize his successes. He went back to work and thrived. He is now a series editor.

It was clear to me when I met Alf that he was doing really well in his career. His bosses had repeatedly praised him and there was no evidence to suggest he was doing badly. In his eyes, he'd failed twice but in my eyes he had done a brave thing in leaving university, changing careers and holding out for something he felt passionately about. I saw this as a sign of strength rather than cause for concern. It's not unusual to try out a few jobs before you work out what you want to do.

Alf's reasons for self-criticism were not unusual. He wanted to do well and he cared deeply about his work. But the self-criticism was causing him more problems than it was solving, blocking his progress and confidence rather than aiding it.

It was my job to help Alf build an argument against self-criticism, so he could see that it was this, not his lack of ability, that was holding him back.

Wave goodbye to self-criticism

Take a moment to think about the pros and cons of self-criticism. First think about the benefits of self-criticism and write them down. Then think about the negatives of self-criticism and do the same.

These were Alf's benefits:

- If I'm critical, it will make me perfect

- If I obsess, I'll know more
- If I make a mistake, self-criticism will ensure that I don't repeat it

When we unpicked these ideas, the reality turned out to be quite different. Rather than helping Alf strive for perfection, he realized that often these negative thoughts played on repeat in his head, making him worry about the best thing to do, taking up time and energy and resulting in avoidance rather than perfection.

The obsessing was the same; instead of helping to counter mistakes it made them feel all the more crushing. It stopped Alf from seeing that mistakes are a normal part of life and something that it is impossible to avoid (we'll look at this in Chapter 10).

My clients often try to claim that self-criticism motivates them and prevents them from being lazy. If you believe that, stop for a second and ask yourself – does it really make you work harder? How do you feel when you speak to yourself in this way? If it makes you feel scared or bad about yourself it's actually much harder to feel motivated.

It's also worth thinking twice about the idea that you'd be lazy without it. Stopping self-criticism won't mean you automatically start slacking. Highly motivated people (you) are still going to be highly motivated if they are nice to themselves. You're not suddenly going to lose everything, slide into inaction and fill your days with daytime TV and pizza.

These were Alf's negatives:
- I avoid bigger goals
- It makes me feel bad
- It takes up too much of my time
- It's demotivating

- It's mentally exhausting
- It is not beneficial for progression
- It makes me discount anything good I do
- It means I don't see the good things going on
- It gives me a false picture of how I'm doing
- It makes me feel angry
- It makes me feel miserable
- Rather than solving the problem it makes everything worse
- Self-criticism is a bully
- It makes me paranoid
- It makes me worry that people don't like me or care about me
- It makes me feel insecure about myself and my abilities

One look at Alf's list confirms that self-criticism is not the helpful motivator people may think it is!

Criticism versus compassion

Look at it this way; if you were training for a new fitness goal and choosing a coach, which one would you go to if you wanted to get the best results?

Coach A yells at you during every training session, shouting that you're lazy, useless, rubbish and a waste of space and time. She tells you you'll never reach your fitness goals, let alone achieve anything and questions why you're even bothering. She rings and texts you between sessions to say how disappointed she is in you and to remind you of your mistakes and failures during the previous training session.

Coach B welcomes you to training and tells you she's looking forward to working with you today. She describes all the improvements she's noticed in you, highlights your areas of strength and points out the areas you still need to work on. Coach B reminds you that it's normal not to find every area easy and that some parts of what you're doing will be more challenging than others. She helps you look at your strengths and shows you how you can use them in other areas. She encourages you to look at what you're struggling with and to work on a different approach. She rings and texts you between sessions to encourage you to keep it up, that you're doing well and to reassure you.

I feel stressed just thinking about coach A. I'd rather hide in bed than turn up to a training session with her. Coach B on the other hand makes me want to try my best and work harder. She inspires confidence and I feel warm just thinking about her belief in me.

Coach A, of course, embodies self-criticism. It's obvious that this person will make it much harder for you to reach your goals and that even if you do reach them, the whole process will be far more unpleasant. It's easy to see that rather than being motivational, this approach makes you feel awful about yourself.

For too long we've believed that self-criticism helps us get things done, when in reality it does the opposite. Even though self-criticism is your own internal voice, rather than that of an external person, the result is exactly the same.

Finally, ask yourself whether these really are the ingredients of success. If we take this a step further and question why you want to succeed — to feel good, to be happy, to gain confidence

– does criticism serve the purpose? I hope it's clear the answer is a big fat *no*.

Coach B's approach is the compassionate approach; it's easy to see that this approach works. Think of compassion as an essential ingredient for life. Compassion will teach you to support and motivate yourself with kindness rather than criticism. So what exactly is compassion?

Choose compassion

When I first talk about compassion with people in my clinic they look a little confused; some even look mistrustful. I think many people have a negative reaction to the idea of self-compassion because self-criticism has such a strong hold on them – they're like two magnets having a face off.

You've been brainwashed by the imposter voice and one of its main tactics to beat you into submission is self-criticism – it doesn't want you even to entertain the idea of compassion. It knows that compassion will be the first step towards criticism losing its key place in your life and eventual defeat. Without its scare tactics you'll be able to hear a different view, releasing the strong hold the imposter voice has on you. Compassion is self-criticism's kryptonite.

I think most people misunderstand the nature of compassion. Having compassion for yourself is really no different from having it for others. It can be helpful to remember that we are not alone in our struggles. No one is perfect, we all make mistakes and it's OK to feel stressed or sad. Pain and suffering are part of our shared human experience; they are just a reaction to what's going on in our life.

Kristin Neff PhD, a pioneer in the field, has defined self-compassion as being made up of three main components:

1. Recognizing when we're stressed or struggling without being judgemental or overreacting
2. Being supportive, gentle and understanding to ourselves when we're having a hard time
3. Remembering that everyone makes mistakes and experiences difficulties at times

A compassionate approach means treating yourself kindly and taking a warm, non-judgemental approach; think brave, strong, fair and wise. These are core ingredients for feeling good about yourself and they are important if you want the best chance of making changes in your life.

Compassion is definitely not soft and woolly, or a way to let yourself off the hook. It doesn't involve self-pity or being self-indulgent or making excuses for bad behaviour. And it doesn't mean thinking positively or only focusing on what's going well while ignoring your faults.

Compassion means recognizing specific examples of our strengths and progress and identifying areas we need to improve. It means taking responsibility for our behaviour – even when it's bad – and accepting ourselves as human. This allows us to see things clearly and stops us getting stuck in repeated destructive behaviours.

It is the perfect antidote to the self-critical and perfectionist thinking that can lead to stress, anxiety and depression. Self-compassion motivates us to make necessary changes in our lives, so we don't continuously judge and evaluate ourselves. We need it not because we're worthless or inadequate, but because we care about ourselves and deserve comfort and understanding to navigate the ups and downs of life.

> *One of my clients, Bella, looked almost disgusted when I first mentioned compassion to her. Having grown up in a family in which emotions were not expressed and compassion wasn't even considered, she had learned to ignore her feelings and had a 'pull yourself together' approach to anything she found difficult in her life.*
>
> *When we first worked together, she wasn't even aware of how horribly she spoke to herself. Her level of self-criticism was at times punitive, leaving her with an underlying anxiety that filtered into everything she did. It was like a game of Whac-A-Mole. She'd tell herself to toughen up and then the anxiety would pop up somewhere else. She never felt she was coping well with life, despite a huge amount of evidence to the contrary.*
>
> *In time, as she came to understand more about what compassion meant and tried it herself, there was no denying what a positive difference it made. It took determination to overcome her old automatic self-critical response, but with hard work she managed it. Her confidence has improved, she's kinder to herself and she's more understanding of other people as a result. Her anxiety has also reduced, making everything in her life much easier.*

Self-compassion is something *everybody* needs in their life. There's a wealth of research that shows it leads to greater happiness, optimism and gratitude. Those who are compassionate are better able to forgive others too.

You will try much harder to achieve a goal if you practise self-compassion – and it has the added bonus of making you feel a lot better about yourself in the process! It helps you feel less stressed, quietening self-criticism. When self-criticism is a bit less loud, you will find it easier to accept and navigate mistakes and failures. This helps you bounce back from setbacks, improve self-worth and become more accepting of yourself.

Try to speak kindly to yourself and offer yourself praise and encouragement as you work through every strategy. Think of the difference your internal commentary can make and choose the frame of mind you wish to navigate the day with.

The two-step process

You should now have a good understanding of the corrosive effects of self-criticism and be ready to embrace a more compassionate approach. Despite all its amazing benefits, self-compassion doesn't come naturally to most people; it takes time and effort and can feel uncomfortable to begin with. To help you bring it into your life, try this two-step process and make sure you stick with it. The more you do it the easier it will become.

Step one: become aware of what you say to yourself

Self-criticism blocks compassion so we need to remove this first. Before you try to upgrade the words you use when you speak to yourself, you first need to become aware of the ones you are currently using. Think of your internal voice as a radio station in your head that says you're unworthy. You need to turn the volume down!

Notice how you talk to yourself – it's usually along the lines of: 'You're useless, you did really badly, that lady gave you a funny look, you stumbled over your words, you didn't even look professional today. You'll never get promoted. No one respects you.' This voice can be quite automatic and often we don't realize we are saying critical things to ourselves.

Try to externalize the voice as you did the imposter voice – the two are pretty similar. It could be another Gobby, a yappy dog, a haggard witch or a comedic figure. Recognize that it's not your voice and you don't have to listen to it.

- Pay attention to what you're saying to yourself. What's your tone of voice? Listen for statements that make you the problem, or suggest that you're not good enough.

- Whose voice is this? If you recognize the voice, is it one you want to listen to? Would you value advice from this person on anything else? I hope the answer is no – it should be.

- Is this voice as helpful as it pretends to be? Write down some of the statements and look at them in black and white. Is this really how you want to talk to yourself?

- When you identify self-criticism, try pausing to ask yourself: is this accurate? Remember it's the self-criticism talking – it doesn't mean you are those things.

- Open yourself up to opportunities, so you start to see all that you are capable of instead.

Step two: find a new voice for yourself

Using new words to talk to yourself is hard and it's natural to feel awkward at first. All I ask is that you give it a try! The good news is that once you start to focus on the positive elements of yourself, your brain is more likely to home in on them naturally. It's a bit like when you decide that you want to buy a car – or a new bag – and you start seeing them everywhere. It's not that there are suddenly more of them, it's that you are tuned into them so you look for them all the time. Our brains are pretty clever when we get them working for us.

Call to mind a person who is compassionate and imagine what they might say. Or think of someone who has motivated you to get something done with their compassionate approach and think about what they said that was helpful. This could be a grandparent, an inspiring uncle, a work mentor or someone well-known you admire. Think about their tone of voice and how they might support or encourage you. It can help to bring an image of them to mind. Are they kind, gentle, understanding? Do they back you to do well? Do they encourage and have faith in you?

Now think about how you can use these ideas to create a more positive narrative in your head. For example, if you've given a presentation that didn't go as well as you'd hoped, instead of launching into self-criticism, try out your new compassionate voice. Say to your critical voice, 'I know you're upset, but you're not helping and you're making me feel worse.' Try to reframe what happened, 'It was hard today, but I did my best.' Everyone gets nervous doing presentations, so say to yourself: 'I'm not the only one and I know I can keep improving the more I do this.' Finally, you could find a way to be kind to yourself: make yourself a cup of tea in your favourite mug, stroke your arm or take a few deep breaths.

As you work through all the strategies in the rest of the book, I want you to commit to using a compassionate approach.

- Be as kind to yourself as you would be to others
- Speak and act kindly towards yourself
- Spend time thinking about what is going well in your life and why
- Take responsibility for your actions
- Be present in the inevitable struggles of life
- Remember what it means to be human – no one is perfect and we all make mistakes
- Accept yourself as you are
- Encourage and have faith in yourself (this may feel a bit weird at first!)

Next steps

This chapter should have firmly disproved your belief that self-criticism is helpful and shown you that compassion is a *much* better approach. This creates another crack in your belief that you are an imposter, so you can loosen your grip on it and hold it a little less tightly.

As each of your arguments is disproved another piece of the puzzle falls into place, in the same way as when you do a jigsaw puzzle. The more pieces you have the easier it becomes to see yourself as you are now, enabling you to update your view of yourself. You'll really begin to be able to see my view once you have most of the pieces in place.

It's OK if you can't be completely compassionate with yourself yet. I'll add more strategies to enhance self-compassion and combat self-criticism as we continue through the book. You need to let go of self-criticism to give the strategies a better chance of working, but you'll also find that you'll need some of the strategies to work on and improve compassion. Self-compassion is a bit chicken-and-egg; it's easier when you feel better about yourself, so it should become easier as you implement the other strategies.

To begin with all I ask is that when you wake up each day you make a conscious decision to use self-compassion. I want you to bring self-compassion to everything you do as you progress through the rest of the book. This will give you a much better chance of understanding my theory and building on these new ideas. It's time to trust in yourself and your abilities.

The next stage is dealing with insecurity and self-doubt.

Chapter 8
Insecurity and self-doubt

'When you feel a bit out of your depth, it can be easy to jump to the conclusion that you're a fraud, rather than seeing that this is a normal and expected feeling.'

By the end of this chapter you should:

- Understand where self-doubt and insecurity come from
- Recognize that everyone experiences insecurity and self-doubt – it's not just you
- Understand that the benefits of insecurity and self-doubt can be harnessed and channelled to your advantage

Now you've waved goodbye to self-criticism and introduced compassion into your life, the next factor I want to tackle is self-doubt. If you think back to Chapter 2 (page 51), you'll remember that when we're in a situation that makes us uncertain it's natural to experience some fear. With this comes the discomfort generated by self-doubt, prompting questions such as: 'Can I do this? Do I know enough? Can I live up to expectations?'

Think about how imposter syndrome operates: it's as though your brain hasn't caught up with your new identity – and confirmation bias stops you from updating your view of yourself. So when you feel a bit out of your depth or uncomfortable, it can be easy to jump to the conclusion that you're a fraud, rather than seeing that this is a normal and expected feeling. This also means that you don't have a chance to build confidence in yourself, which is the antidote to self-doubt.

Extreme self-doubt can generate a mixture of insecurity, uncertainty and vulnerability that can become really problematic. You question whether you're good enough and hold a magnifying glass over everything you do – overanalysing every situation and decision you make and constantly wondering if you could be doing more. You imagine that everyone else knows what they're doing and this thought makes you feel more anxious, thus feeding the cycle of overwork or avoidance.

Instead of recognizing these thoughts as fears rather than facts, you believe them, imagining that you should feel completely confident if you want to take on a task. To disprove the idea that insecurity makes you an imposter I will challenge the belief that everyone else feels OK, that we should feel competent and capable all the time in all areas of our lives and that we should feel good every day.

I'll then look at how to harness the benefits of self-doubt and use them to your advantage.

Self-doubt means I'm an imposter – or does it?

At the core of imposter syndrome is a fear of not being good enough. This might not be there all the time, but when it occurs, you seriously doubt yourself and your capabilities and feel incredibly insecure. To keep this fear in check you believe you should always appear capable, competent and successful. This means you constantly feel you need to prove yourself.

If you don't look and feel these things, you conclude that you must be an imposter and doubt your own worth, wrongly presuming that non-imposters never experience self-doubt or insecurity. In your mind everyone else is managing – they're capable, but you're not.

Self-doubt might drive these fears, but the thought that no one else feels like this is a big part of the problem. And this is where you're completely wrong.

Who doesn't feel insecure at times or worry what others think? If you could read the minds of the people around you, you'd be likely to encounter waves of insecurity. We compare, evaluate and judge ourselves with great scrutiny. It's not something to pathologize, but something we should be aware that we're all susceptible to. In fact, I'm more suspicious and concerned about a person who thinks they know everything. I'd consider those who claim never to experience self-doubt to be more of a problem!

Self-doubt affects *everyone*. None of us really knows what we're doing! How do I know this? Because self-doubt is hardwired into us as an evolutionary protection mechanism.

The evolutionary origins of insecurity and self-doubt

From an evolutionary perspective, insecurity and doubt are part of the 'better safe than sorry' approach that early humans adopted for survival (and a bit like its sibling, fear). An overactive threat detector was a great help in avoiding an early death, so the advantages of self-doubt outweighed the disadvantages and it has stayed with us. Self-doubt and insecurity helped us to be more self-aware, so we could anticipate and overcome potential problems or threats and get on better in our relationships.

It worked to alert us to danger – we scanned the environment for potential threats so we could anticipate problems and avoid accident and injury – and made us cautious when faced with new people, places or events. Self-doubt also helped us judge what we could and couldn't do – if humans had been completely fearless we'd have been an evolutionary quirk rather than the dominant species.

Insecurity is also good for human relationships. We're highly social beings and early humans needed to live together and get on in a group to ensure survival. Being cut off from the group would have resulted in death. This means we have a deep need for social inclusion – we feel rewarded by positive social interactions and hurt by negative interactions. Positive interactions with the same individuals within a framework of long-term and stable care is a fundamental human need and, in addition, the need to belong is integral to self-development (think back to Chapter 4 and how beliefs are formed, see page 74).

Our drive to belong meant that understanding others was a necessary life skill. To allow us to do this the human brain, particularly the neocortex, is much larger in humans than in other primates and mammals. The neocortex is the area of the brain involved in higher social cognition, such as conscious thoughts, language, behavioural and emotion regulation, as well as empathy and theory of mind. This area allows us to understand the feelings and intentions of others and when we have the ability to do this it makes sense that we might at times feel insecure.

As we've evolved, humans have had to be self-aware to succeed. We had to avoid enemies, form useful alliances and find suitable mates, so flawed judgements could be fatal. A bit of insecurity allowed us to get along with others and stay safely in the group.

That need for a sense of belonging is still part of us now and relationships are still key to our health and happiness. Research shows that a lack of social support is as bad for you as smoking. Social isolation is associated with heightened risk of disease and early death, whereas warm and supportive relationships have long-term benefits for health and longevity. Connection is key – relationships are what give meaning and purpose to our lives.

No one feels good all the time

Our level of self-doubt varies throughout our lives and it is normal for it to rise and fall depending on the situation, the people you are with and your mood. It's connected to what we're doing and to the beliefs we hold about ourselves. When you feel confident insecurity fades into the background, but as soon as you feel unsure, it rears its head again.

The imposter imagines that they should always be on their best form, working extra hard and performing in every area to be accepted or to feel they're doing well enough. But no one feels great in every area of their life all the time. We all have our ups and downs. It would be strange to be permanently happy or to always feel confident. Thanks to my work, I know all the strategies and techniques to use to help me feel my best, but I still don't wake up every morning and jump out of bed with a smile on my face!

Much as we may want to feel good all of the time, life isn't straightforward. I think sometimes we forget that *all* emotions are normal. Our mood naturally fluctuates, and we all go through periods of feeling stressed, anxious, irritable or upset. It's completely normal to feel the full range of emotions. We experience the full spectrum because they are all necessary and useful to us.

So-called 'negative' emotions are just as crucial as the positive ones in acknowledging what's happened and making sense of it. No one is capable of breezing through life unaffected, no matter how positive they are.

It's also helpful to remember that everyone else might be smiling and giving the impression they are confident, but they may not be as confident as they seem.

> *Luke frequently compared himself to others, wondering how he was measuring up. All his peers seemed so confident, while he felt the opposite. He felt a daily concern that people would see through the facade and realize there was no real substance to what he did.*

In meetings he worried he would make an idiot of himself. He imagined that everyone else knew what they were doing, that they had it all together and didn't experience the same fears as he did.

Luke felt that his only escape from his feelings was to be promoted; at least then he'd know he was good at what he did and it would put his mind at ease. His boss seemed so self-assured and Luke wished he could be more like her.

Knowing how well everyone else was doing and how hard they were working fuelled his insecurity. He felt a constant need to prove himself, worked long hours and set himself high standards to achieve. He worked harder, read and researched, learned more. His hard work paid off; he scored highly in his reviews and was promoted.

Luke's promotion meant that he worked more closely with his boss, helping her put together presentations and debriefing after big events. It was only then that he saw the other side and how she really felt. In every meeting and presentation his boss looked in control, but afterwards she would question Luke. 'How did I do? What did you think? Did I sound OK?' Luke saw that his boss didn't feel as completely sure of herself as he'd believed and that made him feel a lot better. He respected his boss just as much – maybe more – and this reassured him that you could do well, even when you felt you might not!

Insecurity is exacerbated by the idea that everyone else knows what they're doing, which leads you to imagine that they do not have the same worries, insecurities or fears. Yet in truth, everyone else is not as different from you as you think – as Luke discovered. Even people you are sure *must* be confident feel insecure at times.

They've just perfected the ability to give the impression of confidence; just like a swan gliding along, you don't see them furiously paddling underneath the water.

When you think about it, this is what others see in you too: someone who looks outwardly calm and confident, who has achieved many successes and who can do anything they put their mind to. So next time you're worrying, remind yourself that how you *feel* is not what others see – you're like that swan too.

There are no grown-ups

When you're a child you imagine that when you've grown up you'll know what you're doing and will understand how life works. I think these expectations filter into our beliefs that as adults we should have everything sorted and never feel self-doubt. This idea that we should be competent and capable at all times can pose another problem.

When you think of all the different roles you fulfil – worker, parent, sibling, friend – it can be difficult to keep them in balance. You may have a senior role in your company but can't keep up with the admin from your children's school. You may be the chairperson of a local charity but neglect to check in with your elderly parents. This can make you question whether you really are what others see. When you feel that you're barely staying on top of everything you can't help thinking that if people *really* knew you, they'd have a very different view.

This ignores the fact that it's normal to act differently in different situations or present a public self that is slightly different from our private self in order to meet social expectations.

We do have to put on a bit of a front sometimes; a certain amount of fitting in is necessary and we are expected to conceal our weaknesses, particularly with people we know less well. This doesn't mean we're a fraud or putting on an act.

Everyone sees different parts of us, depending on the capacity in which we know them. I'm a mother, a wife, a clinical psychologist, an author, a friend, a sister, a daughter. How I am at work is a more polished version of myself than how I am at home, with only my children and my husband getting a full view. With good friends I'm very open, but with new friends I filter what I say slightly more. My children's teachers see one side of me and the running club I'm part of see something else. It's normal to modify yourself a bit to fit in with people. Just keep an eye on how much you're doing it and keep hold of an inner measure of who you are, so you know yourself.

No one has all areas covered. Just because you can't keep on top of the school admin doesn't mean you're not a good CEO. You can be many different things and the various parts of you can coexist together. You can feel disorganized and out of control at times and still be an excellent employee and a good son or daughter. You can be tired and short-tempered at times and still be a good partner or friend. You can put your daughter in the bath with her socks still on (like me!) and still be a good parent. Not feeling good or on top of everything at all times doesn't make you incompetent, it just means you're human.

I'm now nearing 40, an age that was defined as *old* when I was younger, and yet I don't feel terribly different from when I was 20. There's no great 'tah dah' moment when suddenly you realize you're an adult. My life is very different, but the change is so gradual you hardly notice it. It creeps up on you instead of announcing itself. You soon realize that adults still feel vulnerable and insecure, but in time you also grow to understand that this is not a weakness, but a strength.

Showing vulnerability is not something to fear, but something to embrace. It's only by accepting all of yourself that you can become comfortable with who you are. Think about the people you feel closest to – do they share their insecurities and fears with you? When they do, what do you think of them?

To me, sharing life challenges and admitting that life can be tough sometimes are the characteristics that make us more relatable, more likeable. Besides, everyone is wary of the person who seems to have everything sorted. They seem a bit intimidating and it's hard to feel close to someone when they project an image of being strong and invulnerable. Throughout evolution our relationships have been hugely important to us, because feeling connected and close to others makes life more meaningful. Don't hide away parts of yourself and create distance from the people who care about you.

You need to put together the many parts of you and see that they all have space to belong together. No one is awarded ten out of ten for every attribute; we all have areas we feel insecure about. You don't have to be a set way to be accepted by others; it's incredibly freeing when you truly believe this. We need to recognize that our idiosyncrasies and flaws make us alive and human. Sometimes our imperfections are the elements that give us our strengths.

If you open up to others, you have a chance to see a different view. We're all winging it and accepting this can be scary in itself. Many of us would prefer to believe that there are grown-ups in control, especially when it comes to running the country, hospitals or law courts!

The upside of insecurity and self-doubt

It's clear that we all benefit from a bit of self-doubt. Humans wouldn't have lasted long without some degree of insecurity. It's easy to see that an element of fear or hesitation is healthy and enhances self-awareness. When you recognize doubt as the questioning part of your brain and ask yourself whether you are OK to do something, you can see that in small doses self-doubt can be helpful. It can offer a way to check and consider what you're doing. A little self-doubt prompts us to operate with caution, to look out for potential problems that might derail us and plan how to overcome them. And the alternative – overconfidence or a lack of humility – can come at a cost to our work and our relationships.

When we think about our evolutionary history it makes sense that we care so much about our relationships and spend time questioning what others think of us. This acts as a gentle reminder that our relationships need our attention, affection and consideration and helps us to monitor our interactions and identify how to get along better in our relationships. Empathy is easier when you recognize your own vulnerabilities and without insecurity you risk alienating others. It encourages us to be humble, grateful and to value what we have.

Insecurity and confidence are not separate but intertwined. It's normal to go from the high of seeing you can do something, to the low of thinking that you're going to fail. Confidence and insecurity are more like a circle, feeding into and leading on to each other.

Self-doubt promotes self-improvement and often comes with conscientiousness, high standards and a strong work ethic. The person who knows it all doesn't see that need and misses out. Uncertainty – another part of self-doubt – means that you acknowledge that you still have things to learn. This drives you to grow and change which is hugely important for maintaining good mental health and improving self-esteem.

In the right quantities, self-doubt is part of personal growth and achievement. Overcoming your insecurities and working things out increases confidence, and when you reflect and hold on to what you've done you can use this as reassurance the next time you feel the same way. The insecurity that drives you may diminish as you succeed, but it never truly goes away. When you see it as part of confidence and finding the right way forward, it's easier to make peace with it and channel it so it works for you rather than against you.

When you feel insecurity or self-doubt raising the volume, find your compassionate voice. It's time to get past the scared child in grown-up's clothes and accept your abilities. Reassure yourself that feeling uncomfortable is something to get used to and that you need to learn to navigate it. Hold on to the idea that others also feel insecure and that no one knows it all; you can use this to challenge the imposter belief.

Self-awareness

There is a fine line between feeling sufficiently insecure to allow you to maintain good mental health and insecurity causing you problems. Become self-aware to avoid this; self-awareness allows you to be aware of insecurity, rather than *being* insecure. Self-awareness means knowing yourself and your strengths and limits, so you feel more confident about what you can and cannot do. There are lots of strategies throughout the book to help you increase self-awareness, identify your strengths and get to know yourself better. But the simplest place to begin is with a daily reflective practice – if you haven't already, it's time to buy that notebook or start making notes on your phone.

Reflection

There's no doubting the importance of reflection. It's a way to understand yourself better, improve mood, learn from your experiences and foster personal growth. Its benefits have been recognized throughout history by philosophers and spiritual leaders and it's the cornerstone of many psychological approaches to improving well-being.

Whether you take time to think about the good stuff that's happening, or the parts of life that are more difficult, or take five minutes to collect your thoughts and put them down in words, it is important to reflect on your life. It's good to look at where you are and where you're headed. This allows you to tackle areas of difficulty and the changes you wish to make, as well as helping you to recognize what's going well and your part in it so you get to know yourself better and increase self-awareness.

We might prefer to avoid the negative emotions such as upset, anger or worry, but you should not be afraid of them. When you try to ignore difficult experiences and feelings, they don't go away. It's like putting them into a big sack; you might not see them so easily, but you're carrying them around with you wherever you go. The more you put in, the heavier your burden becomes, weighing you down and ultimately keeping the feelings with you for longer.

This might seem counter-intuitive, but looking at difficult feelings is the best way to allow them to pass. Reflection helps you unpack the sack and increase your coping capacity. It's not just the act of writing that makes people feel better, it's expressing emotional experiences and learning from what you have done.

Reflection is also very helpful when things *do* work out. Ensure that you take some time to reflect on the good stuff too, rather than immediately moving on to the next thing – this will help you to feel better connected to what you're doing and it's a great way to build confidence in your ability to succeed.

Remember:

- If you don't feel 100 per cent confident all the time, this doesn't make you an imposter
- Be careful about what you expect of yourself in order to judge yourself 'good enough'
- Embrace your self-doubt and see it as a welcome reminder of your limits
- Overconfidence is a problem
- You need to become used to sometimes feeling uncomfortable and to learn to navigate through the feeling. It's normal not to know everything and to sometimes feel insecure

Chapter 9
The pressure to be perfect

'Not aiming for perfection doesn't mean you don't care, or that you're not bothered about success.'

By the end of this chapter you should:

- Recognize that perfection doesn't exist
- Understand the negative effects of perfectionism, and be able to differentiate between healthy conscientiousness and unhealthy perfectionism
- Have some useful strategies for combating the temptation to aim for perfection in everything

Perfection doesn't exist
Perfection doesn't exist
Perfection doesn't exist
Perfection doesn't exist
Perfection doesn't exist
Perfection doesn't exist
Perfection doesn't exist
Perfection doesn't exist
Perfection doesn't exist
Perfection doesn't exist

Look at this statement there in black and white. Take it in. If you're constantly aiming for perfection you're setting yourself up for failure as *nothing* in life is perfect. If you fit the Perfectionist or Superwoman/man competence type you need to pay close attention to this chapter.

Perfection might *seem* possible if you just try hard enough, work longer and do better, but it's really a mirage hovering temptingly just out of reach. You might push yourself on to this beautiful oasis, but what happens when you get there? There's nothing to see, or it turns out to be further away than you thought. Aiming for perfection means that you can never sit still and enjoy the place you are in right now; it stops you feeling content and encourages you to undervalue all you already have as not being enough.

When you question why you feel so restless and dissatisfied, instead of seeing the problem as your drive for perfection, you wrongly conclude that if you just reached a particular goal, got a promotion, did a bit better, *then* you'd feel OK. Your focus is then on the unattainable place you want to reach, rather than the process and learning along the way.

When you aim for the unattainable, you'll always feel you fall short. Add your personal marking system – 'anything less than perfect equals failure' – and you score nil points. When you do succeed, you quickly disregard the success: 'It wasn't such a big deal', 'It doesn't mean much anyway.' If you set your standards so high that you can't meet them and constantly want more you'll never feel satisfied no matter how well you do.

What happens if your success becomes difficult to deny? Your excuses shift to questioning how you will continue with this added pressure. 'I might have done well, but how am I ever going to keep this up?' Rather than not being able to do something you're now confronted with the impossibility of maintaining your progress.

Many people start off with healthy levels of ambition – going for something they really want, passing exams or finding a new job – but somewhere along the line the pressure starts to intensify. When you become very focused and follow an increasingly punishing schedule you neglect everything else. The focus tends to be all on you – you set the standards and you're the one who is disappointed if you don't live up to them. But your standards are impossible to live up to and this is a self-defeating way to move through life.

The sad thing is that even when you do something brilliant, you shift the goalposts that little bit further out of reach. Like the pot at the end of the rainbow, what you want keeps moving over the next hill, something Matilda was all too familiar with.

Matilda had been desperate to get into theatre school. She knew the competition would be tough and didn't dare hope she'd gain a place, so when she was accepted she was thrilled. On her first day, she felt excited, but when she got there and looked around she was taken aback to see just how brilliant everyone else was. She thought to herself, 'I might have got on the course, but it doesn't mean anything unless I get chosen for some good parts.' She vowed to work as hard as possible to give herself the best possible chance.

Every day she hit the gym at 7am, worked from 8.30am to 8.30pm, fixed her food for the next day and went to bed. She did this five or six days a week and her reward was the lead role in the first show. After the performance everyone told her how brilliantly she'd done. All Matilda could think about was that she'd fluffed her lines in the second act. She knew they were just being nice to her – what else were they going to say? And anyway, she probably wouldn't get picked again.

Her time at theatre school rushed by and before Matilda knew it, she was ready to look for her first job. When she was offered a part in a film, she couldn't believe it, but again instead of allowing herself to enjoy the success, she started thinking about how much experience everyone else on set would have and how she mustn't show herself up. No matter how well she did her success never felt enough.

When she met up with her friends, they all wanted to celebrate with her, but instead of feeling happy, Matilda broke down in tears, opening up about her fears and the pressure she felt under. Her best friend turned to her and said, 'Imagine if you told your 18-year-old self what you were doing now. What would she think?' This really took Matilda aback; she remembered that when she was 18 she would have given anything to be doing what she was doing now and, in that moment, she could really see how far she'd come.

Perfection's tight grip

Perfectionism is intertwined with your sense of self and is often about attempting to correct or deal with a feeling of not being good enough – something many imposters can identify with. Achievement can feel safe, it is within your control and can help you manage your external environment and feel good about yourself. The perfectionism comes from pinning your identity on your achievements and serves the function of keeping that feeling under wraps. This makes it hard to leave behind.

While it might help in the short-term, over a longer period this drive for perfection feeds your insecurities, pushing you into overwork or avoidance. If you don't succeed, you don't just feel disappointment about how you did, you feel shame about who you are. Ironically, perfectionism then becomes a defensive tactic to keep shame at bay – if you're perfect, you never fail and if you never fail there's no shame. This becomes a vicious cycle. And because it's *impossible* to be perfect, it's a self-defeating one. How good a person you are is not defined by how many things you can do.

Yet the lure of perfection is like a drug with an addictive hold, telling you it will make you feel better and that nothing but perfection can feel this good. You start with casual use – you might set yourself high standards in your work – but then the addiction enters your bloodstream; you feel a flow of excitement about doing well, a sense of mastery in managing everything and overcoming difficulties which boosts your self-worth and brings a sense of fulfilment.

Once you get a taste for perfectionism, it spills into other areas. You feel a relentless drive to excel, constantly trying to achieve your personal best in your work, your relationships, your home and your appearance. Aiming for perfection feels good initially. If you're good at what you do there is a lot of positive reward, often both financially and for your ego. But even when the results are good, the feeling is short-lived and the happiness is intercepted by a familiar thought – what's next? This diminishes whatever you've just pushed yourself to achieve.

Suddenly you want your whole life to be perfect and you feel disappointed when it's not. Taking on too much brings with it a constant feeling of stress and you exhaust yourself in an attempt to do 'enough' (a measure that doesn't exist). To keep up your standards your life becomes more and more stripped back. Your horizons narrow and you bring a disciplined approach to everything you do, working set hours, exercising, eating the right foods, avoiding caffeine too late, making sure you get enough sleep and trying to stay in control of *everything*.

Productivity feels good and you grow used to the charged feeling adrenaline brings, not just forgetting what it's like to switch off in the evenings and relax, but feeling guilty if you ever do. On the rare times you're not fully in this zone, you just feel tired – really tired.

The messy nature of life means that events very rarely fall neatly into place. Something always causes problems or takes you in new, unforeseen directions – a house, a partner, children or a myriad other responsibilities. Then you always feel an element of dissatisfaction. If you don't reach a goal, your self-assessment can be brutal.

If nothing is ever good enough, this can make life very difficult for a partner, family members, friends or colleagues. You will find it very difficult to trust others or to let them do anything for you.

Even when you manage to, you generally think that they won't do it properly and this creates a distance between you and the people you care about.

Sometimes there is a moment when you meet all your standards. You go to the gym every day, work from 8am until late, eat well, tick items off the to-do list and keep a consistent approach. It feels *so* good! But it's impossible to maintain. The more you reach for perfection the more elusive it becomes as you become less satisfied with what you have done. Maintaining perfection becomes harder and harder and you start to operate at the limits of your mental and physical well-being, competing in an ultra-marathon without an end.

Then slowly it becomes harder and harder to replicate the conditions you set for success. Each day starts to feel suboptimal and you become self-critical, a defining feature of perfectionism. This affects productivity – you waste time on small details, give up on work projects, worry about being judged, avoid taking risks – and this then undermines your potential.

You are held back by the thought that you are not good enough: you need to do better, you need to do more, you haven't pushed yourself hard enough. Perfection might tell you it's being helpful, but actually it's making you miserable. When you're aiming for perfection you'll always be able to find something you can do better than you already are doing it. Yet this idea is something people really don't want to believe.

Why success?

It's human to strive and be ambitious; we're wired to be goal-driven. In evolutionary terms, this makes sense: being happy all the time wouldn't have contributed much to the survival of the species. We wouldn't be driven to achieve, personally develop, meet a partner or reproduce. Having happiness that little bit out of reach is more adaptive as it keeps you moving forward and facilitates personal growth. But there's a fine line between goals that add to your life and goals that make you miserable. And just because we can achieve more or acquire more goals, it doesn't mean we should or that this is the route to happiness.

I want you to stop for a moment and think about why you are aiming for perfection. For most people the desire comes from a good place. Often, we target working hard and doing well as a way of reaching the ultimate goal of happiness, but is it really doing this for you?

In my experience perfectionism does the opposite. It makes accomplishments less enjoyable and gets in the way of appreciating all you already have. What about the external markers of success that you may covet, such as financial success, social recognition and physical attractiveness? They don't make you happy either; in fact they are negatively related to well-being and linked to increased anxiety, depression, narcissism and physical illness. Relationships and time for the things that matter to us are what's most important for health and happiness – the very things that get cut out by a perfectionist approach.

The problem that pretends not to be one

The idea that we can do everything perfectly exerts a pressure that is impossible for us to live up to, but despite its damaging impact the downsides of perfectionism are surprisingly difficult to believe. You don't have to look far to see why. The idea of perfection is celebrated in our society and there is an unhealthy preoccupation with success in our hypercompetitive and results-driven digital age. There's a widely held belief that being a perfectionist makes us better workers, parents and friends. We are valued for what we do, rather than *who we are*.

Social media has made everything seem possible and perfectible, with glossy feeds reinforcing these unrealistic standards. Research backs this up, showing that perfectionist tendencies are on the rise, thanks to an increase in young people's perception of social expectations and the fact that they are growing up in challenging economic and social circumstances. Competition is embedded in schools and universities and competition for jobs pushes young people to focus on their achievements.

Perfectionism is often valued by those who have it; it's not seen as a problem. The combination of sacrifice and success makes it strangely appealing in the same way that the gruelling initiations students go through to gain access to a sorority group make them all the more prized. It's difficult to deny the good feelings you experience, and these reinforce the addictive hold of perfectionism. The function it serves – to keep the fear that you're not good enough under wraps – also makes it difficult to let go of, especially when your feelings of self-worth are based on being exceptional. The secondary gains – a sense of importance, the thrill of working hard and doing well – can blind you to the problems these bring.

Even when you're struggling with long hours of work, when your mental and physical health is suffering, when you *see* the problems that perfectionism causes you and *want* to grind to a halt, the perfectionism ideal calls to you: 'Don't stop – this is what makes you special.' It acts like the sirens in Greek myths, women whose enchanting singing lured men to destruction. Perfectionism convinces you that *you* are the problem, rather than your approach, telling you that your body and mind are failing you, that the work isn't unmanageable it's just that you're not efficient enough yet. But when you are? Glory awaits, and it will all be worth it.

The alternative – life as a mere mortal – isn't so appealing. Average feels boring, scary to even contemplate. Perfectionism gives you a reason to sacrifice your life: 'Other people might not work to these standards, but they're never going to be as successful and are happy to accept less.' You will think of a long list of reasons you need to keep working this hard – you'll miss opportunities, your work won't be respected and you won't do as well as everyone else.

But look closer and you'll see that, like the siren, the glory is not what it promises to be. The daily sacrifices might feel small, but when you add them up, they are undeniable, like death by a thousand cuts. The good moments when the effort feels worth it are fleeting. Exhausting yourself in an attempt to do 'enough' you swing between feeling special and feeling useless and the self-criticism and self-doubt that come with this fuel your fear that you might not be good enough. Imposing these rules on yourself makes the effects more difficult to see. Imagine if someone told you that you had to:

- Work from early until late
- Cut down or cut out your social life
- Stop doing the things you enjoy
- Work when you're tired
- Never take a break
- Constantly push yourself
- Keep going even when you feel physically and mentally unable to
- Miss out on time with those you love
- Work evenings and weekends

When you imagine these demands coming from someone else, it's much easier to see that this way of life is unacceptable.

It's time to

Let. It. Go.

In therapy, this idea petrifies people, but I'm not asking you to stop aiming high. You can still do your best and work hard, but without allowing the effort to become so all-consuming it costs you your health and happiness. You'll still experience the highs of success and hard work as you're good at what you do, but you will only have a chance to discover this if you stop pushing yourself quite so hard.

The imposter voice will scream at this idea – telling you that you'd be mad to lower your standards and accept this new way of approaching life, that you will never be good enough, that you'll miss the satisfaction of doing things perfectly and that life won't be enough without it. So, to convince you I want you to take a long hard look at the costs of this approach.

What is perfection costing you?

Perfectionism is not just unrealistic, it's also costly. Studies suggest that the higher the level of perfectionism, the more psychological disorders you will suffer. And the list is long; perfectionist tendencies have been linked to depression, anxiety, self-harm, social anxiety, agoraphobia, obsessive-compulsive disorder, anorexia, bulimia, binge eating, post-traumatic stress disorder, chronic fatigue, insomnia, hoarding, chronic headaches and even early mortality and suicide. They also negatively affect your relationships.

So stop for a minute and ask yourself – is this approach to life really working for you?

- What are the costs?
- Is it possible to live a life that includes the things that are important to you?
- Can you maintain good relationships?
- Do you have time to do the things you enjoy?
- Is it worth causing your physical and mental health to suffer as you pursue something that doesn't exist?

Aiming for perfection shows an imperfect mindset.

Differentiate

There's no doubt that it's time to change your approach. We will look at this in more detail in Chapter 12, but for now, it's important to differentiate between healthy conscientiousness and unhealthy perfectionism. There's a difference between working hard and wanting perfection. Both might aim for high standards, but healthy conscientiousness prioritizes your health and happiness and uses the carrot approach – compassion – rather than the stick's punishing regime.

Not aiming for perfection doesn't mean you don't care, or that you're not bothered about success any more. It just means you set your standards at a more reasonable level. You can still do your best and work hard without it costing you your health and happiness. Remember the 'let it go' attitude. Let go of this rigid approach to life. Let go of the fear that people think of you in a certain way. Let go of the need to be 'good' and let go of the outcome you're striving for. It's more paralysing to try to become a successful person than it is to spend time doing things you value; it is much better to focus on the process than the end result.

It's easy to become very self-critical when we're striving for perfection – 'This isn't right', 'It's not good enough', 'What was I thinking…' Watch out for overreacting to mistakes and the shame and blame game. Counteract the negative messages and make room for some compassion instead. If something doesn't work out the way you hoped it would, tell yourself, 'I'm disappointed, but it's OK, I'm still a good person overall.' This will leave you feeling very different from when you tell yourself you're a failure and not good enough.

Instead of trying to do everything perfectly, pick a few things you want to do really well. Don't expect to be your best 100 per cent of the time and be flexible in your approach, rather than setting one standard for every area. Rather than trying to evaluate yourself all the time and constantly coming up short, make your goals reachable and take on board your success. To see how far you have come try answering the question Matilda was asked:

'Imagine if you told your 18-year-old self what you were doing now. What would they think?'

- It's good to have high standards, as long as you don't aim for perfection
- It's good to work hard, as long as you don't sacrifice other parts of your life
- It's good to be motivated and show discipline, as long as you don't beat yourself up when you don't succeed all the time
- It's good to do your best, but not if your best never seems good enough and not meeting your goals frustrates you
- It's good to reach your goals, as long as you take time to evaluate them and see how well you are doing

There are rare, but joyful, periods of time when everything feels easy, you get loads done, you can concentrate, you're motivated, you're fun to be around and feel calm and in control. Rather than seeing these times as how you should *always* be, you need to see them as precious, fleeting and golden. Capitalize on them when they happen and make sure you enjoy them, but don't expect them all the time. Rather than criticizing yourself when you're not experiencing those moments, remember that not having them all the time doesn't make you an imposter; it makes you human.

Healthy conscientiousness is a different route to success. It might not offer the same hard-won highs, but I promise that it is *far* more enjoyable. It allows you to keep in mind the fact that you are human and have limits; it's a kinder and more fulfilling approach that allows you to accept yourself as you are *now* with all your strengths, abilities and flaws, so you can get on with living your life.

Chapter 10
The f-word

**'If at first you don't succeed,
try, try again.'**

By the end of this chapter you should:
- Recognize that mistakes and failure are a normal part of life, and not a sign that you are not good enough
- See that mistakes and failure can be used to your advantage, that they make you more resilient and can have positive consequences
- Understand that mistakes and failure are part of any success story

Despite all the noise from your self-criticism and self-doubt, I bet there's a small part of you that thinks you could be not just good, but great. However, as soon as you allow that thought some airtime a second scarier thought comes in. What if you *fail*?

Perfectionism might tell you that it guards against these fears, but actually the two are intrinsically linked. Fear of failure drives perfectionism and perfectionism makes failure seem all the more likely. This fear of failure limits your potential, either pushing you into overdrive – which results in your becoming less focused and effective over time – or making you unconsciously sabotage your chances of success by never really trying. You'll do anything to avoid the emotions of disappointment and anger that accompany mistakes and failure, and most of all to avoid the feeling of shame. While most emotions are a response to our actions (such as regret and anger), shame makes us feel bad about who we *are*. No wonder failure feels so scary.

We need to turn this unhealthy preoccupation with failure on its head and see that mistakes and failure are a *normal* part of doing just about everything and that managing the disappointment that comes with them is a necessary life skill. Not only that, they are an important part of doing well. It's a paradox – our successes are achieved through trying, yet trying often ends in failure.

Overcome your fears

You can learn to overcome your fears, so you are no longer held back by them and they stop dominating your thoughts. You'll better manage mistakes and failures, understand their hidden benefits (yes really) and change your mindset from one of fear to one of adventurousness.

Just to warn you; this chapter will *not* teach you how not to fail. Overcoming imposter syndrome doesn't mean you'll stop making mistakes; it means accepting that they're part of life and that you need to learn how to use them to your advantage. If at first you don't succeed, try, try again.

Step one: accept that mistakes and failure are a normal part of life

It's no wonder you're worried about failure. It's a by-product of self-criticism, perfectionism and self-doubt; they all bolster each other and shout loudly together, making you feel that you're not good enough.

When you think about what you count as failure the odds are stacked against you, thanks to the unrealistic standards you hold. Think back to that shape sorter (page 82); anything negative is caught and held in a great big bucket, while positive things have to be the right shape and inserted at the right angle for them to be taken on board.

The research backs this up. Not only do imposters fear failure, they show greater concern about their mistakes and a stronger tendency to overestimate the number of mistakes they make compared with non-imposters. As you saw in the last chapter, they also tend to be more dissatisfied with their performance and rate it as less successful. It's no wonder that the quieter voice – the one whispering 'go for it' – gets drowned out.

When you do make a mistake or fail, this leads to more self-doubt and self-loathing. You're missing a vital piece of the puzzle, however. No one – and I really mean no one – gets through life without ever making a mistake or failing at one point or another.

Avoiding failure is a bit like trying to avoid common illnesses. The lengths you'd have to go to – avoiding other people, not taking public transport, not touching anyone – require far more effort than suffering the effects of getting ill. You're better off carrying on as normal, putting up with an illness when it inevitably happens and being thankful that it builds up your immune system.

Mistakes and failure are the same. When you make a mistake or fail at something it hurts; sometimes it really hurts. But when you try to avoid it, you're trying to avoid a normal part of life. Without mistakes and failure, you'd also miss their many benefits, which range from learning a lesson to increased resilience.

Step two: accept that mistakes and failure make you more resilient

Although they might not feel great at the time, setbacks do you a favour. Just as common illnesses build up your immune system, research shows that people who have experienced between five and seven major setbacks have a better quality of life and greater confidence to weather adversity. Of course people respond to stress in different ways and some are more vulnerable than others, but what we're looking at is on a small scale. Rather than aiming to avoid discomfort or upset, reframe these experiences as good for personal growth. Even extremely negative stressful experiences can lead to positive psychological outcomes, such as improved problem-solving, optimism, acceptance and a better understanding of yourself as a direct result of experiencing and effectively dealing with them.

These experiences provide you with an opportunity to learn how to cope with difficult situations, helping you discover that they are not as scary as you thought. We all have a mental model of how the world works (think back to your belief system). This allows us to anticipate problems, calculate how to behave in specific situations and work out what we can expect from ourselves and others. We usually try to avoid upsetting or unpleasant experiences, but when we're forced to go through them we gain important information that we didn't have before, which helps us improve our understanding of ourselves and how the world works. The more information our brains have, the better these models are, making our brains better able to understand, anticipate, process and handle negative emotions.

Evidence that the world doesn't fall apart when things go wrong means you will become less afraid of this happening. It also gives you practice in dealing with difficulties, showing you that you can cope.

This knowledge makes success feel more secure, as you're not expecting everything to always go well or worrying about what might happen if things go wrong, so putting less pressure on whatever you are doing. Overcoming challenging situations not only builds resilience, it is also an opportunity to learn.

Step three: accept that we learn from our mistakes and move forward stronger

No one gets everything right all the time. Sometimes you might get things right the first time; at other times it may take several attempts. Even when you've been doing something for a while, the better you do and the longer you do something the more opportunity there is for failure. If you made the same mistake again and again and again, then I'd understand why you'd be upset with yourself, but that's not what happens.

Compare this with learning to play an instrument. Even if you're naturally talented, you still need to practise and work hard to master it; you won't be able to read every piece of music perfectly the first time you try. It would be crazy to think this might be possible. Whether or not you have the talent, you also need the desire to work to develop it.

The path to success is not linear and without failure we can't progress. If your competence type fits with that of the Natural Genius you need to take a good look at this diagram!

The path to success

Remind yourself that you're not an imposter if you don't get everything right first time and that you won't always see improvements week after week. Challenges aren't a sign that you're not up to the task, they are a part of doing anything that's worth doing and just one step along the way to success.

Rather than being full stops, mistakes and failure are part of working out the right way to go about things. They mean that you're not quite there yet. Sometimes you may need to take a few wrong turns before you can find out which the right turns are. The wrong turns aren't wasted time or a signal to stop, but something to learn from. They give you useful information to work out the right way.

You can learn as much from things that went wrong as you can from getting everything right – and if you learn something does this still count as a failure? Making and admitting mistakes is a necessary part of growing and learning and being human. Learning from mistakes makes you more successful in your career and relationships – and life in general. If you avoid making mistakes at any cost, you will find it much harder to reach your goals. When you pick yourself up and look at what's happened you can work out the best way forward.

Success is not innate, but something honed over time. It's important to recognize that talent helps you do well, but practice, experience and hard work are also needed. We need a growth mindset – accepting the idea that intelligence and ability are developed rather than being set in stone. When you look at experiences like this, you're much more likely to keep going in the face of setbacks and to remember that many small steps and much hard work take you to your goals.

If you think about the qualities that are important for success there's no rule that you mustn't ever fail. Instead, one of the key traits is perseverance, the ability to keep going even when you make mistakes or fail!

It's very hard to find an example of someone who has done well without hearing about their failures (and I've looked). J K Rowling, Elon Musk, Oprah Winfrey, Richard Branson, Vera Wang, Steve Jobs, Arianna Huffington, Warren Buffett, Madonna, Michael Jordan, Anna Wintour – all belong to a club you should be happy to be part of when you look around and see the company you're keeping.

> *Bill Gates is a good example of someone whose path to success was not linear. He co-founded his first company at the age of 17. It was called Traf-O-Data and used software to analyse traffic data. Although the company didn't have much success, he and his co-founder Paul Allen used what they learned from that experience to create Microsoft, saying, 'It's fine to celebrate success but it is more important to heed the lessons of failure.'*
>
> *Microsoft wasn't a steady stream of success stories either. In 1993 a database project that Gates thought would be revolutionary didn't work out and Microsoft's TV-style internet shows launched in the mid-90s on MSN didn't succeed. Instead of giving up or slowing down, he accepted the challenges and learned from them, saying: 'Once you embrace unpleasant news not as a negative but as evidence of a need for change, you aren't defeated by it. You're learning from it, it's all in how you approach failures.'*

Every mistake offers us an important lesson, if we allow ourselves to reflect on what has happened. This gives us space and time to process it, reassess, rethink and move forward. When fear of failure feels paralysing and you say to yourself that everything is too difficult and not worth the stress, the opposite is actually true. No one does well without hard work and all the best achievements take a lot of effort, practice and time. The more difficult a task is, the more satisfying it is when you manage it.

While you don't want to make everything in your life difficult, one or two challenges add to the excitement of life. When a challenge is hard, which at times it will be, remember that the rewards will be all the greater when you reach the other side. How good it will feel is something to hold on to the next time you're struggling.

Learning to fail

When you change failure from being a personal failing – 'I'm a failure, I'm not good enough' – to something to learn from – 'I'm disappointed, but I can learn and grow from this' – you feel very different and can let go of shame.

When you think of your previous approach, part of the reason it hurt so much was the post-mortems. You would go over and over and over everything in your head, thinking about how badly things had gone and berating yourself.

- You'd dwell on mistakes and were unable to stop thinking about things that didn't work out
- You'd obsess over the details of conversations, emails or what you did or didn't say

- You'd replay perceived slights, criticisms and tiny errors on a loop
- You were haunted by past failures
- You'd question whether others might be unhappy with you or whether you'd done something wrong
- You'd blame yourself and wish you'd done things differently

Now let's look at the three steps in this chapter again:

Step one: Accept mistakes and failure are a normal part of life.

Step two: Accept that mistakes and failure make you more resilient.

Step three: Accept that we learn from our mistakes and failure.

When you accept mistakes and failure as normal and see them as an opportunity to learn, grow and increase resilience, it is much easier to let go of them. Having followed these three steps, you're in a better position to see this, but the knowledge itself doesn't make everything OK. You have to use this knowledge to actively change how you react to failure.

Next time a fear of failure puts you off trying something, or you make a mistake, use these five techniques to give you the best chance and see things differently.

1. Give yourself permission to fail

If you listen to the imposter voice you'll try to avoid failure at all costs, but this makes failure all the more painful when it does inevitably happen. Instead, think of yourself as a work in progress. Mistakes and failure are part of life. They are going to happen, so you may as well accept them. Approach things knowing that no one finds anything easy when they first try it and remember that you probably won't get everything right first time.

It's normal to find things difficult when you're learning. You can't know the best way of doing something until you've tried a few times. Rather than giving up, try again, work hard and bring in some compassion. Remind yourself that you can get there. It might not be easy, but it will be worth it, and it's the only way to build solid confidence in yourself. If it helps, remember that you're not the only one – it happens to all of us (even Bill Gates) – and remind yourself of the three steps above.

2. Thoughts and feelings aren't facts

Just because you fear you can't do something, it doesn't mean that thought is right. I might feel scared about giving a presentation, but that doesn't mean I can't do it. Remember that thoughts and feelings aren't facts!

When we listen to our anxious predictions and avoid doing something, or give up trying to do it, we don't have a chance to find out the truth. The truth that:

- Our anxious predictions are normally wrong
- The thought of doing something is ten times worse than just doing it
- Even if something doesn't work out as you'd hoped, the consequences are never as bad as you expect

Think about the level of risk and compare this to the reward. The risks are rarely as great or as permanent as you might anticipate and there's so much to gain if everything does go well. Think about what you might miss if you play safe, then be bold and go for it! Going for things you really want *is* scary, but it's very worthwhile. Research shows that we regret what we don't do much more than what we do – so next time you're fearful of going for something remind yourself of this.

Only by really going for something and giving it a proper try will you see you can do it and survive. If you make the presentation you'll give yourself the chance to see that you did well and that it felt good, despite it being scary. The more you overcome these fears, the easier it becomes. This is something you can then remind yourself of the next time you're worried: 'This is how I felt before the presentation, but I was really pleased I did it.'

Watch out for the following thinking biases:

- Generalizing: 'I never get anything right.' Instead try, 'It didn't work out this time.'
- Projection: 'They think I'm useless or rubbish at my job', or another thought. Remember that no one is capable of mind reading – ask yourself whether other people really are thinking these things about you, or are these your own thoughts?
- How you feel is not how things are. You may feel you're not good enough, but that doesn't mean you're right.
- All-or-nothing thinking; one mistake doesn't equal failure. Remember it's a step back and keep it in

proportion – one slip up doesn't mean disaster or that you've ruined everything.

- Magnifying mistakes: you pick out one negative detail and dwell on it. Instead see the full picture – if 90 per cent went well, then spend 90 per cent of your time on the good stuff, rather than focusing solely on what you're unhappy about.
- Personalizing: seeing negative events as something to do with you. You're not responsible for everything – there are many other factors at play!
- Watch your conclusions: compare, 'It didn't go well because I'm an imposter who is incompetent' with, 'It didn't go well because I was underprepared.' There's not much you can do if you believe the first, but you can learn a lot from the second conclusion.
- Hindsight is cruel, telling you that you could have predicted things before they happened. Remind yourself that you can't foresee every eventuality and outcome and think about efficiency. Looking out for every potential problem wouldn't be the best use of your time, especially when you understand that mistakes provide useful information.

3. Reflection

If things don't work out as you had hoped, give yourself time and space to reflect and work through what has happened. Process the emotions, think about what you've learned or consider any benefits that have resulted from what's happened. Often just the act of expressing difficult feelings means you take the power out of them. This helps you make sense of what's happened and offers a way to gain insight into what is upsetting you, making it easier to find a potential solution.

4. Criticism doesn't equal failure

One of the things that can undo imposters is any type of criticism. To move forward you need to manage criticism better and see that it is not personal or character assassination. The comments are about your work, not you. Think about what you do when you give feedback; you don't see the other person as unworthy or inept.

View constructive criticism as helpful. It pays to listen to other people's opinions when trying to improve your work and gain new perspectives. It can also be helpful to remember that the person giving the feedback believes you are capable and trusts that you are able to make changes. You don't have to agree with all the negative feedback – it's just another view. Take what's helpful and let go of what's not.

To get more used to it, try to actively seek out feedback; with practice you'll find it becomes easier and easier. Find someone further into their professional journey who you trust and who can act as a mentor – ideally someone with a similar background – so you can discuss your feelings and share your insecurities. This person should be able to help you separate what's real from your perceptions and offer empathy, advice and guidance about specific areas to improve.

The thought of having someone older, wiser and more experienced looking at your work might feel terrifying, but feedback from someone you respect gives you a chance to see what you're doing right and what you're doing wrong. It can give you a new perspective on your progress and help you develop realistic goals. If you're an overthinker, it also gives you some answers and helps keep these thoughts under control. Done in the right way it gives someone else a chance to understand what you've been through and the effort you have put in and it's a chance for you to see this too.

If you find it difficult to do this, try questioning whether you are over-invested in your work – is it taking up too much of your life and self-esteem? If it is you will find it very difficult not to take feedback personally. If you think this is a problem, you'll have a chance to review your boundaries in Chapter 12.

5. There's no 'right' way

Aiming for perfection offers the illusion that there's one right choice. If there's a right choice, that means there is a wrong choice, and this can be paralysing. You can feel it's your responsibility to do something in the right way and that you'll be at fault if you don't succeed. Instead try to be more realistic – there is no perfect choice; there are many ways of doing things, all of which can be good. And remember that mistakes, failures and 'wrong' choices are not the end of the world. They are part of finding the best way and provide you with more information so you can learn and even grow in the process.

Read these aloud:

- It's OK to make mistakes; they are a normal part of life and an opportunity to learn
- Frustrations are normal and worth persevering with
- I don't need to fear failure
- Resilience is built on mistakes and setbacks
- Nothing ventured, nothing gained

Chapter 11
The myth of lucky and other stories

'With most things in life a bit of luck is involved, but this doesn't void success or make it count any less.'

By the end of this chapter you should:

- Recognize the excuses your imposter voice gives for your success, and be able to expose them as the myths they are
- Recognize and be able to celebrate your achievements for what they are

Our primary focus up to this point has been to change the way you speak and think about yourself, so that you can set more realistic standards and begin to trust in your capabilities. The next step is to help you to see all the good stuff you do. You crave success, but when you succeed, you barely consider the real reasons for it. This is something I'll be aiming to change in this chapter.

You need to remove more of the blocks that obscure your view of yourself and your achievements to take another step towards owning them. This is crucial if you want to overcome imposter syndrome. In this chapter, we'll look at the excuses your imposter voice gives for your success and I'll be exposing them as the myths they are:

- I was really lucky
- It must have been a fluke
- It's just because I worked really hard
- I was just in the right place at the right time
- It's because they liked me; I just charmed them
- It was a team effort
- I just knew the right people

I'm sure you'll recognize at least one of the above, if not all of them. The reality is that almost all of these factors do play a part – who doesn't do well from a combination of these things? But (and it's a big but) as usual your brain is skewing things against you, taking one tiny detail and magnifying it so it obscures everything else. It's like cooking an amazing dinner and claiming that the main ingredient is a pinch of salt. What about all the other ingredients that contributed to the meal?

As well as the list above, there are so many other factors that contribute to success, such as:

hard work perseverance passion
drive **SELF-RELIANCE** curiosity
willpower creativity **patience**
integrity optimism
SELF-CONFIDENCE communication
determination **CONCENTRATION**

Undoubtedly some of your success is the result of factors such as luck or timing, but these make up a small percentage of your overall success. They open the door a crack and provide an opportunity to step in. The external circumstances don't detract from your achievement; you still have to open the door fully, step inside and earn your place there. Without those next steps you won't get anywhere. It's these external factors and your internal resources in combination that create success.

So, let's take them one by one and have a look at their impact and what's really going on.

Myth one: **I was really lucky**

If I had a pound for every time someone has told me that they were lucky to have done so well, I'd be a very rich woman. I hear it on a daily basis and since writing this book I notice how frequently it comes out of my own mouth too. When you say this to yourself, you're not completely wrong. With most things in life a bit of luck is involved, but this shouldn't be the sole focus.

Luck doesn't void success or make it count any less, and if you have luck and don't deserve it, it will soon show. It's knowing how to take advantage of luck that marks you out as different.

A new opportunity, a project that turned out well, a job offer, amazing feedback – these things are not brought about by chance. You don't do well without being good at what you do. It's your own actions that have allowed luck to occur and those who turn luck into something more must have many other strengths and qualities too.

If you take this a step further, is luck really involved when you put yourself in situations which might give you opportunities? Does luck play a part in giving yourself a better chance by doing these things, when many others could do the same, but choose not to? Is luck involved in saying yes to meeting a contact or putting yourself in situations where you might meet people who can make a difference to your career? Is it luck when you do these things, even when you don't always feel like it? If you didn't really want to go, but you went anyway, is that luck? Or is that a sign that you are driven and determined – two key ingredients to doing well?

The luck myth isn't just connected to the way we think about our own success. We also use the idea of luck to make others feel better and to play down our success: 'It's no big deal, please don't think badly of me.' This is based on a worry that success has a negative effect on our relationships. People aren't always happy about others' success and if you're very sensitive to other people's emotions you may find it difficult to discuss your successes. Ambition and striving can be isolating, particularly for women. This needs to change, but that can only happen if we all talk openly about these things, so they become more normal and acceptable.

It's also important to look out for others telling us we are lucky. Some people may find it easier to view your success as luck and so help to strengthen this idea. By looking at it as lucky, they discount the possibility that they might have been able to achieve it, telling themselves that if they'd been lucky they could have done it, but they didn't have the same chance.

> *Carina loved seeing her friend Rose, but she hated any discussion of work. Whenever the topic came up Rose would tell her how lucky she was: 'The stars are aligned for you.' Carina knew she meant it in a nice way and there was a part of her that completely agreed. She did feel that fate had been kind to her, but there was something about it that also left her feeling worse afterwards, as if nothing she had done counted towards her success and that this ignored the long hours and sacrifices she'd made at work.*

It's easier for Rose to see Carina's success as luck rather than something within reach for her too, if she put in the hours and worked hard at it. While she does not intentionally put Carina down, unconsciously that's what's happening.

I hope you can see that thinking luck is one of the reasons you are an imposter doesn't stand up to scrutiny and you shouldn't automatically discount everything you do. It's what you turn luck into that differentiates who is successful and who is not.

Myth one – busted. Luck doesn't disqualify success; it is just one small part of it. It's what happens next which determines whether you succeed.

Myth two: it must have been a fluke

When you feel like a fraud and you do well it's easy as an imposter to deduce that it must have been a fluke. This one is very similar to the luck myth, but while 'luck' tends to be used in broader terms – 'I've been so lucky in my career' or 'I'm so lucky to have such great friends' – 'fluke' tends to be applied in specific instances. Winning a race, being given an award, getting onto a course – it must be a fluke. Then comes the next thought… What if next time I fail? Then people will see the truth! This doesn't just put added pressure on the next time you're in a similar situation, it also takes away the value of your success. Instead of looking at how well you've done, you're busy fortune telling catastrophes. This makes it very difficult to reflect on your success, learn from it and gain confidence.

The definition of fluke is an odd occurrence that happens accidentally and is unlikely to be repeated, rather than being planned or arranged. When you rationally look at the things you are calling a fluke, can you really categorize them as accidental? Even just thinking about how many flukes there have been in your life goes against the definition. Look closer and you'll see it's a throwaway comment to detract from your success instead of seeing the many component parts of what went into making something happen.

Myth two – busted. If you've worked hard and things have come together this does not mean it's a fluke!

Myth three: **it's just because I worked really hard**

Working really hard is another common reason people give to discount their success and linked to this is the idea that if you worked hard and did well, then anyone can do it. As if it only counts if it was really easy!

Hard workers take the initiative, have good ideas and take failure in their stride. They need to show perseverance and be able to listen to positive and negative feedback. They are curious, ask questions and are constantly learning. They go to classes, workshops or pursue further studies. They set themselves goals, work hard to reach them and make sacrifices to get where they need to go.

When you really think about all these things and what's involved, are you sure anyone could have done it? When you do these things and you're used to doing them, it's easy to discredit the effort involved. But there's a reason not everyone does it; it is hard work.

Malcom Gladwell, a staff writer on *The New Yorker*, was nominated by *Time* magazine as one of their most influential people of the year in 2005. In his book *Outliers: The Story of Success* he looked at why certain people were successful (read this book if your competence type is the Natural Genius). His key message, whether it was Bill Gates or the Beatles, is that it was the many hours of work these people put in that made them successful – Gladwell calls it the 10,000-hour rule. Ten thousand hours is equivalent to roughly three hours a day, or 20 hours a week, of practice over 10 years.

Hard work is the only way to do well; no one becomes successful through luck – as the brilliant saying (attributed to the inventor

Thomas Edison) goes: 'Genius is 1 per cent inspiration and 99 per cent perspiration.' When you explain away your success as simply down to hard work, you're not recognizing your strengths.

Myth three – busted. Hard work is the core component of success, not a reason to discount it!

Myth four: I was just in the right place at the right time

Just like luck and hard work, timing is a key component of success, but again it's just one component. Bill Gross is a technology entrepreneur and the founder of Idealab, one of America's most successful technology incubators. Gross gathered data from hundreds of companies to discover which factors accounted the most for company success and failure. He looked at five key factors: ideas, team/execution, business model, funding and timing. To his surprise, he found that timing was the top reason for success and accounted for 42 per cent of the difference between success and failure.

Why is timing important? If an idea comes too late, it will face too many competitors and won't work out. Too early, and certain advances might not have been made to support the idea and make it possible. This is what Gross discovered, when he founded Z.com, an online platform that allowed you to watch videos. The technology at the time was not advanced enough, but, two years later, the problems were solved and YouTube converted the same idea to huge success.

If the timing is right, then your idea can succeed. But how do you know the timing is right? That's where the luck myth comes in. Good timing is not luck. Seeing and recognizing good timing is the skill. Seeing your advantage and capitalizing on it means knowing when to act. It can be easy to look at the time everything worked out and fell into place, but how many other times were there when it didn't?

Myth four – busted. Success is not the result of one lucky strike. Lots of effort means there's space for good timing and everything to fall into place.

Myth five: **they just liked me**

You were one of two applicants on the shortlist; the other guy had more experience, but they chose you as they thought you'd be a really good fit with the team. The imposter's interpretation is that you fooled them into giving you the job by winning them over with your charm.

Hold on a second… You reached the final two and they chose you. I'm sure you had to beat many other candidates to get to that point and, rather than proving you're a fraud, this shows that qualifications and how much experience you have is not all that matters.

I hear the likeability argument a lot in many different guises, especially when someone has been in a job for many years or is facing redundancy. They imagine they've risen up the ranks thanks to getting on well with others and daren't move jobs for fear they will be unable to find something equivalent. Or if they do go elsewhere they worry they will be exposed as a fraud.

This is not just about being the cleverest; how likeable you are is another important component. Being likeable can help to make you a better worker, make teamwork easier and will mean you're more likely to be chosen for a job. You might be incredibly clever but find communication difficult and feel socially anxious – this will make it much harder for you to do your job. Employability is not about one skill in isolation.

Think back to your class at school – the cleverest people may not necessarily be doing the best now. That's because cleverness doesn't guarantee success. Many other factors come into play. Yes, intelligence can be enough on its own, but more often there needs to be more than just this. Often, it's not what you've got, but how you use it that counts. Not being the cleverest doesn't mean you can't do a good job.

Think about the current power of influencers on social media. For them it's all about likeability – that's the key to their success. Does this mean likeability doesn't count?

Likeability is a strength and an important quality for getting along with others. It's definitely not something to dismiss or turn your nose up at. For many people it is something they have learned or developed and it shows social and emotional intelligence, empathy, self-awareness – a pretty strong combo for doing anything in life. I personally see it as a superpower (though as a psychologist I might be a bit biased)!

Those who are likeable tend to be thoughtful and to make an effort with people around them – it means you are interested in others and take time to find out how they are, remembering things about them and regularly checking in. Thoughtfulness and kindness are useful life skills. We all have different strengths and there are many combinations that work well.

Likeability is one part of what matters. Charm and people skills will only get you so far. They might give you an advantage in going for a job or promotion, but you don't get a job just because you're nice; one skill doesn't make interviewers ignore everything else! Most jobs place you under close scrutiny; it would be hard to get through on good acting. Companies have plenty of measures in place, including regular reviews, performance reports and bonus schemes, to weed out anyone who is not pulling their weight. Make sure you acknowledge the other factors at play in success.

It's also important to differentiate between likeability and people pleasing. When you're an imposter you can feel the need to impress those you admire – your boss, lecturer or supervisor, even your partner – and your quest for positive feedback can mean that you're constantly adapting yourself to fit in with others, putting their needs before your own. Yet when you do get the positive feedback you're so desperate for, you dismiss it, believing they're only giving it to you because they like you. Reframe it as seeing that they like you, but they also think you are good at what you do.

People pleasing also makes it difficult to ask for help or to give your true opinion. It is harder to think about your own needs and, in overdrive, it can leave you unsure of what is important to you and what you want. Indeed, the cost of being liked by everyone is that you often don't end up liking yourself very much.

Use your people skills, but make sure you also have your own opinion and feel confident to share it. People don't want someone who thinks exactly the same as them; it gets boring. Contributing ideas and offering a difference of opinion prompts discussion and it's this that often generates new ideas.

Myth five – busted. Likeability does not disqualify success; it's a superpower.

Myth six: it was a team effort

If you've done well as part of a team, then the team will have played a part, but having other people involved doesn't disqualify your success. Be clear about the role you played. There's a reason that being 'a good team player' features on every job advert. It is one of the most important things an employer looks for.

As Aristotle said 'the whole is greater than the sum of its parts'. This idea is particularly poignant when it comes to teamwork, but only when the team is working well. It's no good if you all want to be leaders or follow like sheep. Good teamwork means using your own skills and training (where needed!), listening to each other, taking a lead when necessary and flexibly taking on different roles. It's important to leave your ego at the door and share responsibility. Something many people find very tricky!

It's also important to remember that you don't need to own everything and do everything on your own to do well. In fact this is more likely to cause you to be unsuccessful. I'll be coming back to this one and looking at it in more detail in Chapter 13 (see page 221), but for now...

Myth six – busted. Teamwork is something to be proud of. Being able to integrate into a team and being part of a good team dynamic is not something that comes easily to everyone.

Myth seven: I just knew the right people

So you got your job through a contact: shock horror! That's despicable – or is it? Actually, it's the opposite; 85 per cent of all jobs are filled thanks to networking. Contacts are a necessary and normal part of finding a job.

It's common sense to meet anyone you know who's working in a similar industry when you're looking for a job, whether to seek advice or to find out if they have anything suitable for you or know someone who might. You might even call this approach industrious. You're covering all your options, applying for jobs and making others aware that you're looking.

Using contacts and networking is a well-known and useful approach. There are hundreds of articles about the benefits of networking. Do an internet search based on how to get your dream job and I'm sure this will be one of the recommended routes to move forward. Recruiters recommend it and it is best practice when it comes to job hunting. There's no warning that flashes up: 'Don't do this, it's cheating', or a note that claims that if you use this approach it doesn't count as a real job. It's a practical and resourceful approach! It's what everyone does and if you're not doing it, you're likely to be missing out.

Rather than this approach meaning that you've cheated in some way and you did not earn your position, isn't it good sense to ask everyone you know and to meet them and have a chat?

- If they say yes to meeting you they think you're worth meeting
- If they put you in touch with a contact, they must think well of you
- You still have to get the job – it won't be given to you

If a contact likes you and something comes from the meeting, you've won them over and made a good impression – they have been convinced you'd be a good fit. If they're happy to share their contact book with you, think about why this might be. If they thought you were awful and didn't have a hope they wouldn't put you forward just to be nice. Their reputation is also on the line when they do this.

Let's say your contact is someone who really cares about you – maybe your aunt has arranged the meeting. I'm sure she may have been extra persuasive on your behalf, but no one will take you on out of the goodness of their heart. In fact, in these situations you often have to work extra hard to show you merit being given a chance! The door might have been opened for you, but you are now inside and earning your place there.

If you're self-employed think about how the process works: if you get a new contract through word of mouth, it will be based on your previous work. If you're making a living from what you're doing, then again that doesn't mean you're a fraud.

Let's take it one step further: how many people have good contacts? I'd imagine quite a large proportion of people. But how many of those people have used those contacts and managed to convert them into something more? It's the conversion that's special, not the network.

It's OK to acknowledge connections, but it is also important not to use them to dismiss everything that comes next.

Can you imagine a friend telling you that they are struggling to get a job and then mentioning, 'I do have contacts, but I'm not using them as it wouldn't be right'? It's like suggesting that having gears on a bike is cheating – they are part of how you ride the bike, just as networking is a normal part of work and life.

Myth seven – busted. Using contacts does not disqualify success. Networking and connections are part of maximizing your chances and are known and expected ways to get jobs.

Review how you got here

We're all born with certain talents and we also hone many different abilities and skills as we grow up, whether they are intelligence, sporting ability or likeability. But these on their own don't guarantee us anything – it's how you use them that matters. No one thing makes you competent and there is no single approved route to success.

You deserve to be here. Read that again: you deserve to be here. To remind yourself of this, I want you to:

- Go back to the list of achievements you created in Chapter 4 (see page 85)
- Next to each one, note down what played a part: luck, hard work, timing, likeability, team work, contacts
- Play out what happened in your head. Even if one of these was involved, how have you managed to stay where you are? What strategies did you use?
- Think about what you had to do once things went your way
- Write down the actions you took to take full advantage of these contributors
- Which other skills did you use (refer to the other factors listed on page 185)?
- If someone else did the same, would that make them a fraud?

PART III

HOW TO SAY GOODBYE TO THE IMPOSTER FOR GOOD!

Chapter 12
Reclaiming your life: beating overwork and avoidance

**'It is possible to have
time to enjoy your life and
still be ambitious.'**

By the end of this chapter you should:
- Recognize that it is important to stop overworking and avoiding
- Have some new strategies in place to change the way you approach life
- Start enjoying life and recognize it for the adventure it is

Congratulations on making it this far. You are doing so well and you don't have much further to go. You now understand that you're here because you deserve to be! To completely overcome these problems you need to change the coping strategies you've been using, namely overwork and avoidance. Only when you stop overworking and tackle avoidance will you have proof that you are not an imposter. Now you can end the cycle, trust in this new approach and believe that you don't have to suffer to succeed.

You are good at what you do and don't need to be working as you have been any more. It's time to re-evaluate and think about a new way forward that allows you to enjoy your life.

The old approach

Until now you've been living by the imposters' code of conduct. You've been working hard and treating yourself like a machine. Or you've been running away from your responsibilities and avoiding life. Always on, doing your best, striving, moving forward, or always off, running away, not believing in yourself and hiding from your own potential.

When you're working hard to reach your goals, you give yourself the promise that when you get 'there' it will all be worth it. You tell yourself that once you're 'there' you'll make more time for family, friends or fun. This is like an alternate reality, a place you need to be before you can get on with enjoying your life.

When in avoidance mode – delaying, procrastinating or sabotaging – you tell yourself that there is a future time when you will tackle difficult things head-on. Or that if you wait long enough you'll feel more like doing them.

While this imagined future feels like a good thing, it stops you making the most of today. Life is happening and you're not fully participating. Negative self-beliefs undermine all the good things you have achieved, and there is little room for the things you enjoy.

The worst of it is that you rarely feel that you actually get 'there'. Whenever you become close you unconsciously reset the destination. You can't see how far you've really come and all that you have become.

The new approach

When you accept the fact that this *future* life of satisfaction and contentment won't ever exist, this allows you to make room for another way of being; living a daily life that fulfils you, taking in and *being* in each day. This way will let you live your life *now* and become all you deserve to be. Reclaiming your life is a three-step process:

Step one: reassess
Step two: tackle overwork and avoidance
Step three: start living

Step one: reassess

In the next few chapters, we will reassess your standards and definitions of success. For now I want you to look at how you currently divide your time and energy. Are you realistic about how much you can fit into a week? Write down everything you are currently doing. Include work time as well as time spent eating, responding to emails, time on social media and time for you. Include absolutely everything that is part of a typical day.

Next to each activity write down a time estimate, then add up the total time. Can you really fit all this in? How much time do you have for pleasurable activities? Are you sacrificing your own health and happiness for your work or your relationships? What would it be like to have some boundaries so there is space left over for you?

I know this is a slightly offbeat suggestion, but try thinking about this in terms of animal cruelty: would this treatment be OK for an animal? Say you had a racehorse: would it be OK to exercise and train the horse all day every day and never allow it time to graze, only allowing it to snatch a few hours' rest in preparation for races? Would you get the best from a horse treated this way? If it's not right for an animal, it's not OK for you either.

Letting go of perfection means only taking on a reasonable amount of work and keeping business to a sustainable (rather than burnout-inducing) level. This also works for those of you who suffer from avoidance. Keeping a realistic weekly schedule reduces pressure and makes it easier to work more effectively so you don't have moments when everything feels too much and you grind to a stop – or worse, sabotage what you're doing.

Now take another look at the list and focus on what matters *most* to you.

- Pick only a couple of things that you want to give your time to; everything you say yes to leaves less time for other things, so choose wisely
- Think about what's important to you
- What can you let go of or delegate? For example, is replying to everyone's emails immediately a priority or is guarding your time? It's time to stop doing anything you don't need to do

It's all too easy to overload yourself so your diary never has a gap. But then you're not living; you're just running from one thing to the next, without being present in anything you do.

To think about this, I'd highly recommend watching journalist Oliver Burkeman's TEDx talk: 'How to Stop Fighting Against Time'. He cleverly describes how our efforts to cope with busyness can leave us feeling busier so the majority of us live our lives in a deep state of denial about how finite our lives are (about 4,000 weeks long). He says: 'If we really want to live meaningful lives, if we really do want to make a difference, we ought to try to live wholeheartedly and unashamedly limited lives. We ought to face the fact that we have just a little bit of time here and then focus on doing one or two really important and meaningful things with that time.' The simple reality is that 'you're finite and that the number of things you could have done is infinite'. When we face this fact – that we only have a little bit of time – it is liberating and allows us to focus only on the things that matter most to us.

Your capacity is not infinite, so choose wisely. Time is one of the most precious things there is and it's something that no amount of money can buy. Don't spend it all being busy.

Step two: tackle overwork and avoidance

The only way you will really see what you're capable of and start to trust in the fact that you are not an imposter is to stop overworking and avoidance. This will feel scary and will initially leave you feeling exposed, but the short-term pain will give you an amazing long-term gain.

You need to do less. If you work too hard, I'm sure you won't like the look of this. But only doing less will help you see that your work is good enough – and you'll be more likely to enjoy it too. The standards you set for yourself are far higher than the standards others set for you – trust me on this. Your 'good' is seen as 'excellent' by others. And the irony is that many of your colleagues, friends and family are all in the same boat – finding it easier to spot the excellence in others than in themselves.

Instead of aiming for 100 per cent aim for 80 per cent and stop agonizing over the last 20 per cent. To test this out, start handing in work when you consider it 80 per cent done. See what others think about it. Or if you're someone who feels they need to do three extra hours of work at home every night and to work weekends, experiment with not doing that for a week. Or doing half that. Break the imposter cycle by putting in the work and effort that a particular project deserves based on its merit and difficulty level.

When I suggest that people do this in my clinic, they usually find that cutting back makes little difference – no one notices (or cares) that they're working differently. The extra time they have for rest or pleasure can even improve their performance.

I know this will be hard, so try thinking about it in terms of efficiency. Doing everything perfectly is not an effective use of your time. Think about it: is the extra time you spend stewing over tiny details really worth it? How many projects have you thrown away because they weren't perfect, or because you worried about how others would judge them? Work doesn't need to be completely 'right' before you share it. Getting something out is better than abandoning your hard work. When you're too close to it, you don't have a clear view of it – let someone else have a look and remember that perfection is the enemy of greatness. Progress, not perfection, is what really matters.

To work in a more reasonable way, it's also important to be more transparent about your life outside work. Rather than saying yes to everything and letting your personal life suffer, be honest about what else you are doing. If you have to leave early to pick up your kids, say so. If your wife is unwell and you need to look after her, be upfront about it. Search for common ground with your colleagues and build bonds where you can – knowing you can share information and advice and rely on each other makes a big difference. It will also let you see that you have nothing to hide. They see all of you and they do not see an imposter. If there's more transparency you can begin to change your life and you won't feel that the two sides of it – work and home – are so separate.

To stop overworking you need to:

- Make yourself a priority
- Set boundaries at work
- Don't always put others' needs before your own
- Take breaks
- Say no
- Delegate
- Stop micromanaging (it's horrible for others and you)
- Be open and honest
- Keep a firm grip on your diary; don't let requests and commitments pile up

If you can stick to these points you will free up a lot of time. Doing this will also change the cycle, so you have a chance to see that you are doing well.

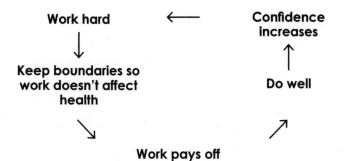

The more you do this, the easier it will become and the feeling of not pushing yourself to destruction is also reinforcing, helping you to stay on track. The next stop is overwork's evil twin, procrastination.

While overworking leaves you too busy, avoidance also eats into your time. Picture the scene. You have an important task you want to complete today. You sit down to start work, but you decide to quickly check your emails first, to get them out of the way. While you're at it, you may as well check whether you have any social media updates – then before you know it, you've played a game on your phone, put on a wash, checked the contents of the fridge and made a cup of tea. But you haven't even started your work.

Does this ring any bells? We're all guilty of putting off chores or unpleasant tasks from time to time and it's understandable that we are tempted to put off things that aren't much fun. But procrastination doesn't just affect the things that don't matter. Often when we have something important to do we can feel a bit anxious. We dread having to do the task, so we ignore it and do something that makes us feel better.

When your level of fear is higher it is harder to self-regulate, so when a task is challenging you switch to something you don't fear doing, tempted by instant gratification, rather than tackling long-term goals. There's no doubt that fear of failure and perfectionism also play a role. You put off the inevitable, preferring to be judged for lack of effort than ability. You may find it impossible to start because you want to do everything perfectly, obsessing over the best approach.

Procrastination might feel like an escape, but it leaves you feeling much worse and wastes your precious time. It also blocks your potential, makes you miss important opportunities, prevents you reaching your goals, has a negative effect on self-esteem and is linked to stress and anxiety.

You can also procrastinate when your mind needs a break. Why not choose when you do this so you can have a brain break that will enhance your life, rather than frittering away time without any satisfaction?

The usual advice is to get on with something, which isn't terribly helpful. If the task was that simple you wouldn't be procrastinating in the first place! Here are some ideas to help overcome this problem, so you keep time for the things that *are* important to you. Try reminding yourself how good you'll feel after you've completed the task. Although procrastination might delay feeling bad, it's only temporary and in fact you'll feel worse in the long run, as you add stress, shame and guilt to the mix. Instead, think about how you'll feel once you've completed the task.

You also need to remember to be kind to yourself; don't forget self-compassion. This might sound strange, but research shows that one of the most effective things you can do is forgive yourself for procrastinating. Procrastination is linked to negative feelings, so if you reduce these through forgiveness, it puts you in a better position to do well next time.

Don't wait until you feel like doing something. One mistake procrastinators tend to make is to hope that a time will come when they will feel like doing a task. This time is unlikely ever to arrive. The best thing to do is just to get started. Even if you don't feel like it, you can still get it done.

When you think big, the next thought is to wonder how you are ever going to do something so demanding. If you look at what you need to do today, it becomes more manageable. Monotask: focus on one task at a time and be realistic about how much you can achieve – most things take longer than you expect. If the task is big, break it down into smaller components. Just starting will make you feel that you can do it, increase self-esteem and give you the confidence to keep going.

Delay gratification: instead of rewarding yourself before you start work, try doing it when you've finished. Try working for 45 minutes then checking emails for 15 minutes. Switching tasks is also good for productivity.

Keep distractions out of the way. If you're on a diet, you don't keep cookies in the kitchen. Turn off social media updates, log out of your email account and close the door to everything outside the task.

Finally, get in touch with your future self. Make sure you're really clear about why you want to do what you're doing. How will it make things better for you in the future? Why will you benefit? Make your goals concrete and think about what you'll gain if you reach them.

Remember that even with the best of intentions everyone procrastinates sometimes. The gap between what we say we'll do and what we actually do is bigger than you think. Think of all the people who join a gym with great intentions, but then never go. If you do procrastinate, don't use this as something else to beat yourself up about.

Avoidance can also make many imposters risk-averse. Focusing on what you know feels safer than being too optimistic, making mistakes or taking chances. Some risk avoidance is normal and healthy – if you narrowly miss being hit by a car when crossing a busy road, choosing to cross at the traffic lights from then on is a proportionate response to reducing risk. However, deciding never to cross a road again would be a disproportionate response. You might then start doing increasingly absurd things to avoid an activity that is perfectly safe in an appropriate context. As an imposter you could think about this in terms of avoiding negative feedback, failure or trying new things. You'd rather maintain the status quo and keep things running smoothly, but this means you'll miss opportunities to progress and the riskier choices which hold the potential for greater gains.

Going forward it's important not to avoid risk at all costs, but to be flexible in your approach. Think about what you think it's worth taking a calculated risk to do, based on the lessons you've learned so far. We'll look at stepping out of your comfort zone in Chapter 15; this is a great way to push your limits and open up opportunities for yourself.

Step three: start living

Previously, you did not give yourself permission to relax and enjoy yourself. But now, you should have a bit more time to consider bringing some balance into your life. Pleasure and relaxation might previously have felt like dirty words, but that is about to change. It *is* possible to have time to enjoy your life and still be ambitious. You can let go of that old belief that equated having time for yourself with being lazy.

This might sound obvious, but the first thing you need to do is to look after yourself. This means eating well, drinking enough water, getting plenty of sleep and exercise. These are the foundations of a good day.

It's important to be more generous with yourself, not just in terms of these basic needs, but in working out what truly makes you happy. Time for meaningful activities, self-care and compassion are key to feeling good. Rather than seeing this as wasted time, see it as time you're investing in yourself. It's not selfish to care for yourself; it's necessary, especially if you want to keep doing as well as you have been.

How we feel is the product of all our choices, especially the small choices that each of us make every day. If you have no time to rest or reflect you'll drive yourself into the ground. If you don't make time for the things that naturally boost your mood, you'll find it difficult to feel good. While you wait for the big things you'll miss out on all the great little things that happen every day. You need to appreciate all you already have.

To gain real satisfaction you need to make three simple changes: slow down, empty time and focus on natural highs.

Start by taking every day a little more slowly. When you're travelling at 100mph it's hard to enjoy life. When you slow down and switch out of autopilot you can take things in. Rather than waiting to achieve a goal, try to appreciate what you already have in your life by practising gratitude – this strategy is great for cultivating a positive focus and it changes the way we perceive our lives in such a simple way.

When we think about what we're grateful for, we force our minds to focus on the good things we already have, rather than dwelling on what we don't have or searching for something new. This has so many benefits – people who are grateful are happier, healthier and more fulfilled – and it's also easy to do. Plus, when we feel grateful, we're better at appreciating and noticing other areas of our life that evoke gratitude; it's a practice that grows and one that offers a lasting route to happiness.

Next you need to allow yourself some empty time. We used to have downtime naturally built into our day: time to look out of the window, to daydream or feel a bit bored. Now almost every moment is taken up with looking at your phone, answering emails or paying bills. You might think you're putting the time to good use, but that's not how your brain interprets it – it needs breaks in tasks and concentration and if it's constantly bombarded it becomes overloaded. Use this argument to remind yourself that all time does not need to be productive. We don't need to be constantly doing or thinking – we're not machines. Even if you are meeting your standards at present, this is not sustainable.

Our culture makes refusing things difficult – what if the opportunity doesn't come again? Don't we need to be living life to the full? In short, no! You do not need to say yes to everything! Learning to say no is an important life skill. You need to adjust your expectations to appropriate levels and abandon a machine mentality – sometimes to do your best you have to start doing less.

If your time is so full that you don't have a moment to sit back and take it all in and you're too tired to enjoy it, what is the point? Rest and recovery are essential parts of a healthy and happy life. For example, plan a morning with no specific focus or simply do one thing at a time rather than three at once!

Finally, you need to make time for the things you enjoy. I call these natural highs. These are what make you feel alive: your favourite music on loud, running, being outside, doing well at work, cooking an amazing meal or being part of a performance. Natural highs are our relationships, loving and being loved, giving back or being part of something bigger than us.

Tuning in to natural highs and working out what makes you feel alive is also a great way to replace the need to aim always for perfection. Achievement is not the only way to feel good! Rather than chasing the satisfaction you get from everything turning out exactly as you want it to, look for the great things that surround you every day. Rather than hurting yourself and those around you by trying to bend the world to your will, accept it for what it is and appreciate its everyday brilliance, even if it doesn't meet your definition of perfection.

Now keep this chapter in mind and take a moment to think about what you want for yourself. It doesn't need to be complicated. This is not about finding a perfect formula or even having a set way of doing things. It's simply thinking about engaging with your life and the people you care about. You need to ensure that you listen to your body and mind and keep your eyes open so you can appreciate the world and all its beauty and wonder.

- What might be a more reasonable way to live your life?
- How can you slow down?
- What can you do to allow yourself some empty time?
- What could you include in day-to-day life that you enjoy?

These ideas don't need to be set in stone; try them out and see how you get on. I suggest that you should always reserve the right to change your mind. If something is not working, look at it and make a change if you need to.

Live life as an adventure

Remember that life is not a race to reach your goals. I like to think about life as an adventure, something to experience rather than a mountain to conquer. It doesn't matter if you stop along the way or veer off course – you're exploring. This is why it is so important to gain as much as you can from what you're doing, to learn and make mistakes. It also gives you a chance to listen to your thoughts and feelings, look after yourself through the journey and adapt the adventure based on the moment.

Goals might form the foundations of the adventure – the reason for setting out – but strange as it sounds, reaching your goals is not important. It's how you get there. You don't have much control over becoming something, but you do have control over how you spend the most important resource in your life – time. Focusing on the process brings meaning and greater happiness. Success is a by-product, not something to strive for.

Chapter 13
Adjusting your standards

**'No one has all the answers.
I think that's a good thing.'**

By the end of this chapter you should:

- Recognize that it is impossible to know *everything*
- Understand that it is alright to ask for help, seek advice from others or collaborate with colleagues
- Recognize that, sometimes, not having the answer can be a real strength
- Trust in your abilities and have confidence in what you do know

You should be clear by now that everyone feels like an imposter to some extent. We are all human and we all have a degree of self-doubt – everyone experiences insecurity and lacks confidence at times. Now we've looked at overwork and avoidance, I want to dismantle the idea that you need to know everything and that success only counts if you create it on your own. Experts and Soloists, listen up!

So far I've looked a lot at the cognitive biases you hold against yourself – the idea that you don't know enough, that you're not smart enough, that you have fooled everyone into thinking you are more capable than you really are. Although I'm still very keen for you to change this view of yourself, I want to show you why, in actual fact, it is a sign that you clearly are up to the job. To do this, we need to look at the Dunning-Kruger effect – a cognitive bias in which people believe that they are more intelligent and capable than they really are. It's the opposite to the bias you hold.

Psychologists David Dunning and Justin Kruger conducted four studies and found that participants scoring in the bottom quartile on tests of humour, grammar and logic grossly overestimated their test performance and ability.

In their paper 'Unskilled and unaware of it: how difficulties in recognizing one's own incompetence lead to inflated self-assessments', Professor Dunning noted 'the knowledge and intelligence that are required to be good at a task are often the same qualities needed to recognize that one is not good at that task – and if one lacks such knowledge and intelligence, one remains ignorant that one is not good at that task'. Teaching the participants skills to improve their scores on the tests also helped them to develop greater self-awareness and their self-assessment improved.

Essentially, people who are incompetent at something are often unable to recognize their incompetence. This means that just by worrying you're not up to the task, you're showing greater self-awareness and self-knowledge.

Let's take learning a language as an example. Your friend has planned a trip to France, and so decides to learn the French language. Before he starts, his confidence in his French ability is extremely low – he understands nothing and the task ahead of him seems extremely daunting.

However, after a few weeks of learning, he realizes he now understands a lot of French words. He is even able to have an entire conversation in French. His confidence soars, and he decides that learning a language isn't difficult at all – he is practically fluent! This is the Dunning-Kruger effect. Your friend is a long way from being an expert and knows only conversational French, but he believes he is more capable than he really is.

But if your friend tried to write a letter in French, or read a difficult French novel, he would quickly come to realize how much more he has to learn. His confidence would probably plummet, despite the fact he understands far more French than he did before he started. It would only be through continued study, and more understanding, that his confidence would begin to increase again.

This applies to many things in life. After an initial surge in confidence, we suffer setbacks and experience disappointment. The more we learn, the more we realize that there is a huge amount we still don't know and that learning is infinite rather than finite. But as we overcome these setbacks and continue to move forward, our confidence can begin to increase again. While we might not know everything about life, we grow more confident that we will be able to deal with whatever comes our way.

We continue learning throughout our lives, and to me, that's one of life's greatest gifts.

There are a lot of advantages to early confidence. I think we need to believe that we can successfully take on challenges and this youthful optimism means we try to obtain the things we want. Imagine if you'd known how hard life was going to be when you were younger – the stress of finding a job, renting or buying a house, or the way your life changes when you have children. You need belief and confidence so you don't miss out on all the brilliant experiences that come as a result of striving for these things.

For the imposter, the trigger point is the realization that they don't know everything, and this makes them wrongly conclude that they must be a fraud. Your mood also affects how much you feel you know and whether you can see your progress. Fear and low mood make you feel less confident and more insecure, while feeling good makes you feel more confident. What I want you to understand is that it's impossible to know everything and if this is the goal you set for yourself you're resigning yourself to feeling like this for life. Try to think of someone who knows everything. I hope you're unable to, but if you think you know of someone, are you sure that they never ask for help or look things up or tell you that they'll come back to you on something?

No one has all the answers. I think that's a good thing. I also want you to see that the discomfort that comes with not knowing everything is not a bad thing. By now you should recognize that this is not proof that you are an imposter, but a feeling that everyone experiences when they step outside their comfort zone, and you should be able to respond to it in a different way. Reframe it to see that it's possible that being aware of these fears allows you to be more open to learning and means you're more curious, helping you progress and evolve. This can motivate us to learn more, question and grow and this is what helps us thrive, something we'll be looking at in the final chapter.

Starting a new role

If you're a student, trainee or apprentice, you have signed up to learn and be taught. Think of these job titles; they are not professor! Take advantage of being a student or trainee. You're not expected to know everything. How could you possibly when you haven't had an opportunity to learn yet? No one is expecting you to arrive as the finished article; what would be the point of doing the course? You will be a better student and easier to teach if you don't know all the answers! When I was a trainee clinical psychologist this made such a difference to me.

If you've been given a new role it's not because people think you're the fully formed article, it's because they see your potential. When you take on a new role or join a company remember that you're new and you can't know everything about it yet. Your colleagues will expect you to learn on the job and grow into the role. It takes a good three months to know your way around a new place; six months will pass before you settle into a daily routine; and it will probably be a year before you really feel at home.

Instead of thinking that you should know it all, see yourself as a learner:

- Be honest about what you know and don't know
- Practise saying, 'I don't know, let me come back to you on that'

- Look things up
- Seek advice and assistance
- Ask questions and accept help
- Go to workshops. Attend training courses and conferences
- Treat yourself with compassion and be patient

Tell yourself that you'll work hard to learn a role; this feels empowering. Remind yourself:
- No one knows it all
- This is new to me
- I'm making good progress
- I don't have the skills yet, but I can grow into the role
- No one expects me to be an expert immediately
- All I need is an eager approach and to make sure I'm ready to learn

If you wait until you know enough to feel ready, you'll wait a long time. Not knowing everything is not a good reason to delay.

Confidently hold a position of knowledge

Even if you hold a position of knowledge or you have been in a role for a long time, you are not expected to know everything. The idea of knowing everything is very restrictive. If all the great minds thought they knew everything, no one could advance and there would be no exhilarating leaps of faith.

Whichever sector you work in, it will be constantly evolving and changing. If you take pride in your work and want to gain satisfaction from what you do, aim to continue learning in your role and be comfortable with this idea. If you don't know the answer, admit this and say that you'll find out!

Think about:

- What if someone says to you 'I don't know'? Is this a bad response?
- To be an expert do you really need to know everything?
- Are the rules you apply to yourself and the rules you think appropriate for everyone else different? Is it all right for your boss to show he doesn't know what he's doing sometimes because he's so good at what he does?

Help and collaboration

The important question is: do you know enough to work out an approach or an answer? Knowing what you're doing doesn't mean knowing everything; it means understanding some of it yourself and being prepared to find answers to the stuff you don't.

- Can you use your knowledge to look in the right direction for answers?
- Do you know how to find answers to the questions you don't know?
- Do you know where to look for information?
- Can your practical skills help you work out answers?
- Do you know people who can help?

Support, help and collaboration don't cancel out what you do – they are part of doing well. Maisie was the perfect example of this. Despite doing well, she didn't think she was very good at her job. This is what she told me when I worked with her.

> *I don't understand why they think I'm so good at my job. I think I'm well regarded at my work; everyone seems to like me, but I don't know why. I don't really do anything. I just get on well with my colleagues – it's not difficult if you talk to people. I recognize people; I know who they are. I'm just playing the game. I think I'm favoured as I'm nice and smiley and blonde and I'm in a male-dominated industry. I don't know any of the answers; I'm just good at finding out. I get away with loads as I play on being a girl; I wouldn't be where I am or get away with all I do if it wasn't for that.*
>
> *I'm a sham – I rely on other people. I don't know very much about making decisions. I just know who to speak to. It's logical; anyone could do it. I'm just asking questions and I get other people to do the work. Somehow I always get it done. Then I get people to think they want what I'm suggesting. I make them believe it's their idea and as a result they're more receptive to it. Really, it's another trick. Other people create documents, case studies or PowerPoints, but I just talk to people.*
>
> *There was a problem at work this week and they asked me to look into it. I didn't know the answers, so I checked some websites, spoke to a few consultants and went to people in the company who are important. Then I came up with an answer. They think I did loads of work to find it, but I don't think I did enough and sometimes I doubt that the answer is right. I might have missed*

stuff. There might be people out there I don't know about. Or I might have asked the wrong questions.

I think I also sound like I know what I'm talking about because if you tell me something once I'm good at remembering it, but I'm just repeating what's said to me. I'm a confident parrot. None of it is my work or ideas.

In my last company they thought I was really good, because they were a backward company and were completely non-reactive. It was nothing to do with me being good.

For success to be special I'd have to put in a lot more effort. I don't do enough. I'd understand if I did a lot more work than I do, if I had more output. I could do so much more if I just streamlined my work, but I'm constantly procrastinating. I fritter away time on social media. My work rate is about 10 per cent.

I work a four-day week and always get results, but it's because I speak to people. People were trying for years to persuade a branch of the company to come on board with a new way of working. They wouldn't budge. I was asked to get involved, so I spoke to everyone and found out what their concerns were. I listened to them and worked out what they needed.

I then organized a workshop and invited all the relevant people so they could personally answer the questions. The finance director got in touch afterwards to say that it was such a good session and that she now understands it and is fully on board.

The head of my team came over and put his hand on my shoulder. He said, 'You're amazing, I cannot believe you've got them to agree to it', but I just got all the right people in the right place at the right time. I just speak to them like they're normal, rather than being scared of giving an opinion. It was nothing special.

Adjusting your standards   223

All the above shows that sometimes not knowing everything is a strength! It ensured that Maisie went and talked to people when something needed doing. This is why there are experts in different disciplines; you don't need to reinvent the wheel every time.

After time and consideration, Maisie and I came up with some challenges to her estimation of herself.

- I'm not a girl! They see me as one of them, otherwise they wouldn't take me seriously
- The company spends millions on work as a result of my recommendations
- I know who to speak to and researching and problem-solving is a strength
- Putting information together and remembering it isn't easy
- Distilling key ideas and problem-solving is not something anyone can do
- Everyone procrastinates at times; it doesn't mean they're not doing a good job
- No one has 100 per cent productivity
- Forming good relationships at work is important in any job

We thought about Maisie's role as being like a project manager on a house build. The project manager might not knock down the walls, install the electrics, plaster or decorate, but they know the right individuals who will get the work done to a high standard and they know how to get the best out of their workers. Being able to do this is a skill and not one that is easy to come by!

Be realistic about your strengths and weaknesses

If you're trying to do everything on your own and feel that the work is piling up, step back and recognize that if you can't manage, it's not because you're not working hard enough, it's because the amount is unmanageable. Doing well means knowing how to get the job done, but it also means knowing your own limits.

You can feel that you have little choice, but that's another lie to keep you trapped in the cycle of overworking and perfectionism. If things are not working, you need to change them. People will have more respect for you if you know how to do something without making yourself ill. And if you work for yourself, you need to sit down and work out what you really want.

If you work for a company, then speak to your boss. Discuss what is realistic; if you don't do this, they may take advantage of you. The company will appreciate you speaking up, rather than suffering in silence. If you feel that you're not listened to, don't fall back into the belief that you're not good enough, but think about what your options are. These are difficult choices, but this is your life. You will not be given a medal for doing it all on your own.

Your health is not replaceable. You have a responsibility to yourself to manage how much you are doing and to take care of yourself. No one else will do this for you and they shouldn't have to. You're an adult and capable of seeing these things for yourself.

- It's OK to ask for more time
- It's good to ask your boss to help you prioritize what's important if you are being given lots of work
- It's OK to ask for more information if you're unclear what is needed

- It's OK to ask for a bigger budget or more resources
- It is essential to value yourself and your health

Bluff!

While it's good to be open and honest about what you know, there is also room for some bluff. The key is to understand that this is a natural part of getting by in life and doesn't mean that you are essentially not good enough. You can imply that you know what you're doing, even when you're not completely sure. It's what everyone else is doing! They don't always know what they're talking about, but they can give a good impression of knowledge even when they don't have it. They'll go for a new challenge even though they don't feel 100 per cent ready. They'll apply for something even if they don't have every skill listed on the job spec. They're no more qualified than you; they're just more confident in themselves.

It's time to trust in yourself. You have good experience, so trust your instincts and go with them. It's OK to have a few theories and not be sure which is right. Pick one. You can then build on it and gain more information to see where to go next. This is just one tool in your whole kit; it doesn't mean you should act as though you know everything and never ask for help but you should see occasional bluffing as normal and recognize that this doesn't make you a fraud. You can improvise a bit and grow more comfortable with not knowing. And sometimes you don't realize quite how capable you are until you step into unknown territory or take a leap of faith.

There's a difference between bluff and dishonesty. You're not trying to get by in a profession that you know nothing about. You have the core skills and understanding to build on and do the job. Trust in your ability to work everything out. You don't need to *know* everything before you start, but believing in yourself will help you to gain trust in your abilities and move forward in your life to a much better place.

Repeat after me — *you can never know it all*. Nobody in the whole world knows everything.

Chapter 14
Boosting your mood

**'A daily approach makes
a difference when it comes
to caring for our minds.'**

By the end of this chapter you should:
- Recognize that your anxious predictions are rarely correct, and that worrying about them is neither helpful nor productive
- Have strategies in place to combat anxiety and low mood
- Be able to visualize success
- Be starting to live in the moment

Your achievements are the result of your talent and hard work. I hope this simple message has hit home. I want you to cement this new view of yourself, so you inhabit everything about who you are and firmly believe in your capabilities.

In the final two chapters, I want you to think about the best way to maintain these new insights and remain vigilant for any signs of the imposter. I'll introduce some new coping strategies to replace the old ones we've dismantled which will put you in the best position to move forward with your life.

As we saw at the beginning of the book, in a strange way imposter syndrome is part of a survival strategy of self-doubt that navigates us away from potential risk or failure, makes us work extra hard and means that we never rest on our laurels. It has got you so far, but I hope you're now fully aware of both the sacrifices you've had to make and the limits the syndrome puts on your potential achievements and your appreciation of them.

With all these new insights, you're now in a better position to identify times when the imposter voice is at work, but it's also important to be proactive in looking after your mental health. When you're busy, it can be all too easy to think that if you just keep going until life becomes easier, your mind will take care of itself. Or that looking after your mind means doing something big: taking a holiday, enjoying a day at a spa, changing your job or moving to a different country. In fact a daily approach makes a difference when it comes to caring for our minds. When you feel good, it's much easier to hold on to everything you've learned and to put it into practice.

Although you might feel that happiness is the result of what happens to us, research proves that as much as 40 per cent is linked to our intentional daily activities and the choices we make. Only 10 per cent of our happiness is affected by external circumstances and the other 50 per cent is thought to come from our genes. This means that you can actively work to keep your mind strong, which not only makes you happier, but also protects against the imposter voice.

For me the small everyday things are the most important when it comes to looking after myself. These can make a huge difference to mental health. The following strategies are designed with this in mind, so they are easy to fit into your life and become part of the proactive approach.

In this chapter we cover anxiety and low mood and in the final chapter we'll look at confidence. Try out all the strategies so you have a menu of options for dealing with these problems when they strike.

Anxiety

Imposter syndrome rules through fear, and when you are afraid it is much harder to keep in mind everything you've learned so far. When you feel anxious you experience anxiety both mentally and physically. Your mind whirrs and the fight-or-flight response kicks in. This combination of adrenaline, increased heart rate, living on high alert and in a constant state of tension leaves you on edge. These feelings further confirm to you that everything is *not* all right, increasing anxiety further and keeping the cycle going. To keep the imposter at bay and regain control you need to bring your anxiety level down. Here are five techniques.

Remember that feelings pass

Hold on to the idea that anxiety is normal and can be helpful. It's the result of your body responding as it should and it is designed to protect you. On a basic level it alerts you to danger. Feelings of anxiety are an understandable response to being outside your comfort zone, rather than a sign that you are a fraud or that something is badly wrong. They prepare you for what's ahead, concentrate and sharpen the mind, remind you what's important and motivate you. The aim is not to eliminate anxiety altogether.

Anxiety might not feel very nice, but it can't damage you. Anxiety does not increase infinitely, but reaches a peak and then comes down again. Knowing this puts you in a stronger position, and you can use the knowledge to bring compassion to the way you're feeling as a way of reassuring yourself when you next feel anxious.

Remember that feelings are a bit like clouds; they're not permanent but around for a while before moving on. Although we might prefer what we term 'good' feelings, all feelings are valid and experiencing the full range of emotions is what makes us human. When you have darker feelings remember that how you feel does not necessarily reflect how things are. We are not our feelings and we have a choice about how we react to them. Remind yourself that these feelings are not permanent and that the sun can break through.

Don't believe anxious predictions

One study asked people to write down their worries. They were later asked to identify which of their anxious predictions came true. About 85 per cent of the worries were never realized. Although 15 per cent of worries were realized, 79 per cent of these respondents discovered either that they could handle the difficulty better than they had expected, or that the difficulty had taught them a lesson worth learning. In other words, their worries didn't really come true either.

If you add together this group of people with the original 85 per cent whose fears weren't realized, we can see that the worries of 97 per cent of people in the study did not come true. This proves that our anxious predictions are rarely correct. Remember that 97 per cent of your anxiety is your mind conjuring up events that are unlikely to happen. And even if what you worry about does happen, worrying about it beforehand rarely offers you any tools to deal with it. To prove this to yourself, over the next week keep track of your worries using a table similar to the one below. Write down what you plan to do, then record any anxious predictions, followed by the outcome and how you coped.

WORRY OUTCOME DIARY				
Action	Anxious prediction	What was the outcome?	Better or worse than predicted?	How did you cope?
Starting an important piece of work.	It won't be good enough and I'll get negative feedback.	I procrastinated, but when I got it done everyone was happy with the work.	Better.	I completed the work within the time frame.
Chairing a meeting.	I'll say the wrong thing and make a fool of myself.	I was nervous, but no one noticed, and I enjoyed being the chair.	Better.	I was really pleased with how I did and I'm glad I put myself forward for the role.
Performance review.	I'll get negative feedback.	The review went better than expected, though I did get some negative feedback.	Better.	I was disappointed but reminded myself that all feedback is part of learning.

Completing this table will give you a chance to update your predictions and see what really happened so you can take this on board. You can also use it for future reassurance – the next time you feel you can't do something, call to mind a time you doubted yourself but went through with whatever was worrying you. What were you worried about? What steps did you take that you think made a difference? When you feel more confident, take it a step further and start purposely testing out your fears.

Use the mind–body link

Changing how you feel physically is another easy way to settle your mind. What we think has an impact on how we feel physically, but the opposite is true too. The brain and body are constantly sending messages to each other and work together to look after you and keep you healthy. When you think about your favourite food, your mouth waters. When your stomach is empty, it tells your brain that you are hungry and need food. So you can also use your body as a route to feeling calmer.

When you experience a fight-or-flight response, you may not actually need to run away or fight off your stressor, but your body will respond as if there is a need. Your heart rate increases, breathing gets shallower and shifts into the chest, you grow hotter and your muscles tense – to name just a few responses. Reversing this reaction using a slow breathing technique shifts you away from the stress response and calms your nervous system. Breathing also offers a whole host of other benefits for your body and mind.

Your breath is an anchor; it's with you wherever you go and is a really simple way to feel good. Try 4-7-8 breathing to make the mind–body link work for you:

- Place one hand on your chest
- Place the other hand on your stomach just below your ribcage
- Breathe in slowly but deeply through your nose for a count of four, allowing your stomach to push out your hand and feeling your chest rise
- Hold the breath for seven seconds
- Breathe out slowly through your mouth as quietly as you can for eight seconds. Feel your stomach move in and your chest drop
- Repeat three to five times

When your mind feels overloaded, it can be easier to tune into your body. If you don't find breathing helpful, find something that does help. Exercise works brilliantly to reduce levels of stress hormones in the body. It stimulates the production of endorphins, which increase feelings of relaxation and optimism. There are loads of other options: muscle tension and relaxation, imagery, yoga, Pilates, or whatever works best for you.

Manage uncertainty

One of the main triggers for anxiety is uncertainty. The trouble is that when you're anxious you're more likely to question yourself and this doesn't help. Think of the moment on TV quiz shows when the host says to contestants, 'Are you sure? Final answer?' Usually a contestant's belief that they know the right answer disappears or is significantly lowered. The more they question themselves, the less certain they become because doubt breeds doubt. Rather than being helpful, too much questioning and analysis make you feel more uncertain! So what's the alternative?

You can never be 100 per cent certain, so rather than trying to become surer, the best way to manage this is to increase your tolerance of uncertainty. Modern life doesn't give you many opportunities to practise this; everything is instant – you can email and get an immediate reply, find the best route using a map app rather than risk a traffic jam, or watch a full box set so you don't have to wait to find out what happens. As a result, we have little experience of uncertainty or not knowing something. Try to find ways to experience not knowing, such as checking your email only twice a day or spacing out the times between watching episodes of a box set. The more you practise the easier it becomes. It's also good to remind yourself that uncertainty isn't something bad, just something you don't know the answer to yet.

Visualize success

Our brains often focus on rehearsing everything that might go wrong, but spend very little time thinking about what could go right. Imagine you have a big event or job interview coming up. If you're feeling fear, you're already mentally rehearsing it in a negative way. When you imagine worst-case scenarios, you feel the same emotions and physical responses as you do when something negative actually happens.

Instead, try preparing for success. Next time you prepare for something important, rather than running through worst-case scenarios visualize your best possible self. Athletes and actors often practise this technique before competing or performing. It encourages both their minds and bodies to recreate exactly what they have just visualized. Picture yourself experiencing all the possible positive outcomes of an event so you see, hear and feel success rather than failure.

Visualize your best possible self:

- Picture the most confident version of yourself you can imagine: you on your best ever day
- You will be confident, sound knowledgeable and speak clearly so see yourself looking confident and imagine feeling bold
- Physically echo the posture and stance of this version of you. Lower your shoulders, stand tall and keep your chin up
- Run through exactly what you want to happen – every last detail – in your head. What does this confident version of you say, do, think and feel?
- Watch yourself succeed exactly as you'd like to
- Run it through again and keep practising!

Mood

If you want to stay mentally fit, the next adversary to overcome is low mood. When your mood is positive, this broadens your thinking and makes everything feel more possible. When your mood is low, everything seems harder and this can prevent you remembering who you are and what you're capable of. Try these strategies and make a mental note of which work best for you.

Avoid self-scrutiny

It's easy to assume that everyone is paying close attention to your life, but the reality is that most people are more interested in themselves. They are not necessarily negative or selfish, but just preoccupied with their own lives and their own insecurities and fears. The idea that you're an imposter has never crossed their minds and it can be helpful to remind yourself of this.

The scrutiny we subject ourselves to is completely different from the scrutiny we give others. I remember attending a singing group with my son in which the leader would sometimes get down on the ground and scuttle around like a crab. It never crossed my mind to think that if it were me I'd feel really self-conscious. I just watched and thought how much the kids loved it! I'm telling you this to help you hold on to the idea that no one really cares much about what you do. Even a man scuttling around on the floor like a crab doesn't raise an eyebrow.

Knowing that others aren't playing close attention gives you the freedom to go for the things you want without being afraid of what others think.

Speak up!

Keeping the above self-scrutiny arguments in mind, I want you to get used to saying what you think. When you suffer from imposter syndrome you fear that you're going to say the wrong thing or that you will be caught out. You feel comfortable with your ideas when they're in your head, but as soon as you say them you worry that they will be judged. You imagine that everyone will spin round and focus their attention on you. But this is not the case.

Think about being in a meeting in which different people speak: how hard do you scrutinize them? Or do you just take their opinions as valid contributions? Even if you think they're wrong, how does this change your opinion of them? Not much I'd guess. If you thought they were wrong and judged them for it at the time (it happens sometimes) how much longer did you think about it after the meeting? Did this make you question everything about them? Again, I'm guessing not. You probably didn't spend any more time thinking about it.

Tell people your opinion. Offer your thoughts. Speak up in the next meeting you attend. A mixture of thoughts and ideas make a meeting more interesting. It's good to question the status quo, and differing options are vital for any organization's plans or projects to succeed: you need people who can think through gaps, point out any issues, anticipate potential problems and make ideas better, stronger and more likely to reach fruition. If in doubt, ask a question. If you don't understand the topic under discussion, the chances are that a few others in the room don't either. Finally, when you do speak up don't hide behind an apology – when you constantly apologize for yourself, it shows that you see yourself as inferior.

Avoid making comparisons

Imagine this scenario: you arrive at a networking event because you've decided to get out and meet potential clients in person. You have a stack of business cards to give away and you're ready to impress. But then, you're not. As you meet other people at the event and hear about their work, your work feels lacking in comparison. When you compare yourself with others, it can be easy to talk yourself out of feeling good, but it's not your work that is the problem, it's imposter syndrome.

We have a drive to evaluate ourselves – our attitudes, abilities and beliefs – and to do this we often compare ourselves with others. This can be helpful, but you need to make sure that you don't make assumptions about others that aren't necessarily true, such as that they are clever, they never doubt themselves, they're managing everything or they have self-belief.

This way of comparing is unfair: we hold up the best parts we see in other people, cherry-picking from everyone we know, without taking in the whole picture of their lives. From this we invent a way of being that we believe we should follow, which can leave us feeling that we're not good enough.

Social media can feed this; it promises to make us more sociable and connected, yet it can make us feel inadequate and judged. We can be selective in what we choose to show others, opting for perfectly cultivated lives through censored sharing. And although we're only showing our best bits, we forget that other people are doing the same, so comparisons creep in.

Try not to fall into the comparison trap:

- Be aware of comparing the way you're feeling inside with what others show you on the outside. Often the image we portray is very different to what we feel underneath. Remember that you can't hear what's going on inside other people's heads.

- What you see is only part of the story. On social media, in magazines and at parties, you see people at their best, but this is not the whole story. You never know what's going on underneath the surface.

- Remember that no one has it all together all the time. *No one.*

- To get the most out of social media, make sure you connect with people whose opinions you value. Surround yourself with supporters and connect with people who lift you up. Actively engaging with others through the platform is much better for your mood than being a voyeur.

- Next time you catch yourself comparing yourself negatively, *stop*. Often these thoughts happen automatically so we're not aware we're indulging them. By noticing when they strike, we have a chance to act.
- Rather than comparing yourself with others take pride in what you do.
- The best course of action is not to compare yourself to anyone at all! We're all different and someone else's successes or failures don't reflect on you. Use them for inspiration or motivation, not as ammunition to beat yourself up.

Remember to switch off

We're becoming ever more connected through technology. The first thing many people reach for in the morning is their phone. You've only just opened your eyes and you're pulled straight into a world that's not yours: other people's lives, your work, the news and all the pressure, comparison and expectation that brings.

Thanks to blurred lines between work, social life and home we can fill every second; we're rarely without our phones, laptops or tablets. Pings, pokes, likes and follows are the currency of modern life. We even check them on the toilet! Whenever you're working, checking, updating or replying you're 'on' and being constantly in this state is exhausting. At it's most severe, it can also be a form of avoidance as it's so absorbing it allows you to ignore the other stuff going on in your life.

Technology is an incredible tool, but it's essential to put some boundaries around it if we're going to get the best out of it. Make sure you give yourself breaks from technology and be aware that it can have a negative impact on your mood and sleep. It also eats into your personal time.

Ask yourself:

- Is this how I wish to spend the majority of my free time?
- Map out a working day for yourself; decide on your work hours and stick to them – it's amazing how quickly people will respect these hours if you are disciplined about this. The same goes for being on holiday
- Keep your phone out of your bedroom
- Think about how you wish to spend your time (look back to Chapter 12)
- Log out *at least* one hour before going to bed

Try mindfulness

When your mood drops you can dwell on the negatives, on anything you are unhappy with. Thinking, planning, having a busy mind or focusing mainly on worries and problems can become a habit, allowing you to go over and over a problem without reaching any conclusions. At these times it can be easy to shift away from the reality of what's going on around you and listen to what's going on in your head. All the emotions, memories and physical feelings associated with these negative thoughts will come up, as though you're living through them.

Watch out for the stories your mind tells you and remember that they are just that: stories, not facts. Thoughts can't change the future or unpick the past, so when you find yourself dwelling on something, try to notice what's happening. Ask yourself how you feel. If the answer is 'not good' then stop and shift your attention to something else. Tell yourself that this thinking isn't getting you anywhere and try to actively shift your focus, so you escape from your thoughts and return to the world around you, whether to make a cup of coffee, ring a friend or go for a run.

Try to become more aware of what is happening around you now. Mindfulness is a great technique to help you practise noticing what's going on right now in the life you're living rather than thinking about a past that's gone or a future that's yet to arrive. A simple starting point for mindfulness is to pay attention to the world around you.

Use all five senses:

1. What can you see?
2. What can you hear?
3. What can you touch?
4. What can you smell?
5. What can you taste?

When you're listening to music pay attention to the different instruments playing, the lyrics of the song and how the pitch changes. Really listen to sounds you can hear in the room and outside. Look around you; what can you see? What colours are there? Where is the light and where is the shade? Think about textures and whether the objects around you are hard or soft, ridged or smooth. How would they feel if you touched them? When you eat your next meal, pay attention to the food. What does it look like? How does it smell? How does it feel in your mouth? How does it taste when you bite into it?

When you try to be in the moment, you'll find that even when you look out, your mind may be pulled back inward. It's normal for this to happen; our minds naturally wander and this is an old habit you're trying to break. Just observe the thoughts and then refocus your attention on the present moment. Today is the only day you can do something about, so it's important you're *in* it!

Next stop confidence!

Chapter 15
Becoming comfortable with yourself

'Being comfortable with yourself and confident in your abilities is the ultimate protection against imposter syndrome.'

By the end of this chapter you should:

- Recognize your achievements, strengths and skills
- Have strategies in place to combat your old imposter excuses
- Be starting to reflect on the good things in your life, be it work, personal or social
- Be celebrating your accomplishments!

When you feel confident, life is so much easier. Confidence helps us back ourselves, reach our goals, try new things and believe in our decision-making capabilities. It helps us manage stress, feel self-worth and deal with problems. It's the ultimate antidote to imposter feelings.

At the moment, the way you see yourself is still lagging behind the way you really are. You have not saved all your achievements in your confidence reservoir, so that when you hit fresh problems, you don't have a confidence store to fall back on. Now you can see that you've come to the wrong conclusion about yourself, I hope you can also see why it's time to recognize your achievements and properly change this outdated view.

If you want to see all of yourself, rather than the five per cent you're unhappy with, you need to start looking at the full picture of your life. Now the imposter belief is no longer in action, confirmation bias cannot operate in the same way. This means you can move forward without the old cognitive biases that have held you back, but you are still likely to be out of practice in taking on board and internalizing your achievements. This chapter will put that right!

Think of this as a confidence boot camp. I'll be introducing you to lots of strategies and you'll have to work hard. But this is the way to get you started on a new path of thinking about yourself and treating yourself better.

Internalize your achievements

I want you to build an inner measure of how you are doing based on *everything* you have done. Be honest with yourself about what you know and have accomplished. This will give you a more stable and accurate picture of yourself, so you can see how well you're doing and take ownership of all you have achieved so far. You will also become better at recognizing your accomplishments and your role in making them happen.

When you internalize your achievements, this gives you a log of everything you have done, so you know your capabilities. You can assess what is needed and look at your experience to see if they match. I think of this as similar to the way top tennis players are seeded; it's an equation of all their previous performances which gives them a rank. If they win a match, they don't automatically become the number one seed, and if they lose, they don't crash down to become the lowest seed. The seeding takes on board all their matches to give a true picture.

Moving forward you will be able to recognize your strengths and connect to them, so you are no longer reliant on external validation to feel good about yourself. This will allow you to enjoy your successes, build self-esteem and gain confidence in your decision-making. You will learn to trust your instincts and new challenges will seem less daunting.

Don't worry, I'm not encouraging you to be arrogant. You're so far away from this that you can shift up significantly and still be a long, long way off. However, I do want you to build a healthy confidence in yourself, based on an accurate reading of your abilities and having trust in yourself. To do this, you need to take a four-step process:

Step one: Take on board your achievements and recognize your strengths.

Step two: Acknowledge your role in these and recognize what it means.

Step three: Become better at seeing your strengths and successes in action.

Step four: Step outside your comfort zone.

Reviewing your achievements (see Chapters 4 and 11) has been the first step towards this. Your external excuses have been discredited and this brings your internal qualities to the fore. Now is the time to look at all you have done and (finally) take on board your achievements!

Recognize your strengths

Start paying attention to your strengths, skills and the qualities that make you unique.

Take a moment to think about your good qualities:

• What good qualities do I have?

• What good qualities have I shown in the past?

• How might others describe me in a positive way?

It can be hard to name these qualities, so use the list overleaf as a starting point and expand it to suit you. If you find the task difficult, ask friends or family, or try a strength questionnaire (the online VIA Survey of Character Strengths is a good one and it's free, see page 281).

accepting assertive **capable** caring
CONFIDENT determined
down to earth **efficient** **empathic**
enthusiastic **experienced** fit FRIENDLY
funny gentle **HARD-WORKING**
honest **insightful** intelligent LOGICAL
loyal **mature** nurturing
OPEN-MINDED optimistic patient
PERCEPTIVE practical **quick thinking**
REALISTIC **reliable** resilient
resourceful **responsible** serious **strong**
supportive thoughtful **trustworthy**
versatile willing

Once you've identified your strengths, assess which you relate to or identify with most. Try to narrow them down to five. Ask yourself how often you use these five strengths and when you tend to use them most. Are there other areas in which you could use them? From now on try to notice your strengths and pay attention to what you're doing well; try to be aware of using one of your strengths every day.

Tell me more

Next, ask your friends and family to write down your good qualities and send them to you. Try to ask at least three people – ideally more. This is something I ask people to do as they near the end of therapy and they always cringe at the idea, but I promise it's worth doing. The session when we go through what everyone has written is always really special and this process makes such a difference to self-belief. Usually there are lots of overlapping themes and it feels amazing to hear what others think of you, especially when this contrasts with how you've been seeing yourself.

Summarize your key strengths and skills

Look back at the lists you created in Chapters 4 and 11 (see pages 85 and 197). Now I want you to add the strengths you have identified and then the feedback you had from friends and family. Next write a list of all the reasons you deserve your job or relationship or pay rise – whatever is appropriate for you at the moment. Why might your boss think you're capable, worth promoting or deserve a pay increase? Add the reasons this shows you are not a fraud. You can refer back to this when you feel anxious.

Finally, decide on your key strengths and skills. When you look at everything written down, are there some key ideas that stand out? People normally find the same ideas come up again and again and some core themes emerge. Are you hard-working? Loyal? Creative?

Write a list of your five key strengths and skills, entitled 'My Key Strengths and Skills'. Take in what you've written and see that *this* is the real you.

Take note of the good things

Now you have a fairer picture of the past, I want to ensure that you bring the same approach to your day-to-day life. We rarely spend time dwelling on the good stuff; when life is busy it can be difficult to give this the attention it deserves. We have a natural focus on what goes wrong in our daily lives and often go over and over the elements we're unhappy or anxious about or that we're finding difficult.

It's important to remember that you have a choice about where to direct your attention. Notice the everyday things that make you feel good, rather than waiting for big successes or wishing time away. Thinking about the good things will have a positive effect on your emotions and confidence, leaving you feeling physically energized, upbeat and calmer.

To shift your focus, start noticing and writing down the good things that happen to you every day. Put effort into thinking about your positive experiences, no matter how small. This creates a virtuous circle; once you start looking for these things the more you'll see. Write them down in your notebook or on your phone every day. They can be anything that is going well or that you're pleased about – work, personal or social. Spend five to ten minutes at the end of the day reflecting on all the good stuff you've noticed.

- Keep track of all your achievements and celebrate the little things no matter how small
- Pinpoint anything that happens that makes you smile or feel good
- Take compliments on board
- Stop minimizing achievements
- Record your role in making things happen
- Accept praise without giving excuses

Reflect on why the good things happened. Your reasons will make you see the world – and by reflection yourself – in a more positive light. Look back at your lists at the end of the week and give them the attention they deserve.

The people I work with often find compliments a stumbling block. One way to deal with this is to think about the impact on the person who is giving you a compliment if you dismiss it. You're saying you don't consider their opinion valid and that you know better, when they're trying to say something nice to you. Have you ever been in a situation when you gave someone a compliment and they dismissed it? It doesn't feel great. When you are given a compliment say thank you and write it down!

After a difficult day, reflecting might be the last thing you want to do, but as soon as you start something will come to mind and it ends the day on a better note. On the days you're feeling good it's nice to relive some of those moments and think about them again.

Walk the walk

You can use the mind–body link to increase your confidence, particularly when it comes to your posture. A study published in the *European Journal of Social Psychology* found that participants who sat up straight in their chairs rather than slouching were more confident about the things they were then asked to write down. The study discovered that posture builds a sense of strength and confidence in social situations too. Power posing has also hit the headlines thanks to the studies Amy Cuddy completed at Harvard University. She found that those who sat in a high-power pose felt more powerful and performed better in mock interviews than those who did not. The idea of 'fake it till you make it' really does work!

Remember the answers to old excuses

OLD EXCUSES	NEW WAYS OF RESPONDING TO SUCCESS
I got lucky. It was a fluke.	Luck doesn't disqualify success; it is just one small part of it. It's what you do next which determines whether it becomes a success or not.
I'm a good actor.	No one is such a good actor that they can keep up an act at all times. Your competence is part of who you are; it is not an act.
I fooled them.	You underestimate other people! Don't forget that concrete evidence backs this up – assessments, reviews, goal setting – these can't be fooled.
It's because they like me. They're just being polite.	Likeability does not disqualify success; it's a superpower. No one will keep you in a job just because they like you. Likeability, charm and the ability to get on with others is an important part of success. It will make you a better team member, boss and employee.
It was nothing. It sounds more impressive than it is	Remember to keep realistic standards; if people think something sounds impressive, it can't be nothing. It's important to count the good stuff rather than focusing on negatives.
I had a lot of help.	Knowing what you're doing doesn't mean knowing everything; it means understanding some of it yourself and being prepared to find out the answers for the stuff you don't.
I just worked really hard.	Working hard is a skill; it requires perseverance, determination, concentration and the ability to acquire knowledge and learn. This is not something that comes easily to most people.
If I can do it anyone can.	This is absolutely not true. It's important to see that something has gone well because *you* have done a good job – you have strengths and talents and it's important you own them.

I was in the right place at the right time.	You need to know when to act, see your advantage and capitalize on it. It's easy to look at the time everything fell into place, but how many other times were there when it didn't? Lots of effort goes into making sure timing works and everything falls into place.
They have low standards.	Did you believe this before you applied? Who else has got in and how do you view them? Offering you a place doesn't mean an institution has low standards.
They've made a mistake.	Universities, courses and jobs have rigorous interview and application procedures.
They felt sorry for me.	No one gives someone a job or a place on a course because they feel sorry for them.
It's positive discrimination.	Positive discrimination doesn't trump suitability for the job. If it did, there would be a far more equal split across jobs when it comes to gender, BME and LGBT+ groups.
No one else wanted to do it.	Really?
It's only a matter of time before I'm found out.	There's a reason you haven't been found out so far: there is nothing to find out. The discomfort you're experiencing is a feeling everyone has; it doesn't mean you're an imposter.
I had connections.	Using contacts does not disqualify success. Networking and connections are part of maximizing your chances and are known and expected ways to get jobs.
I look good on paper.	Only people who have done well look good on paper. Take in what's written on the paper – you have achieved all this!
I interview well.	Interviewing well is a skill, but your interview is not the only element. Employers also look at your background, experience and qualifications and will take up references.
It's an administrative error.	Have you ever heard of this happening? I haven't.

It must have been a weak year.	What proof do you have of this? Is it a thought or a fact? If you underprepared and still did well, recognize that this shows you are bright and good at working under pressure.
I was on the reserve list, so they didn't really want me.	You made it to the reserve list; this is the list of people they want but don't have immediate space for!
They mixed up the marks.	Highly unlikely! Wouldn't the person who got your mark have something to say about it? Remind yourself you're doing well.
They let in the wrong person.	How could this happen? Think of all the checks that occur. Remember you can do it and that they are lucky to have you.
I picked an unpopular course.	Whatever the course, educational institutions are selective and you still have to complete the course to pass or qualify.

Celebrate your accomplishments

Celebrate your accomplishments and reward yourself for doing well, not after you have seen how you've done, but for succeeding in the first place. If you've won a new contract buy yourself a gift, go out for a meal with someone you care about, buy something for your home or book a massage – whatever feels like a treat to you. All too often we move on to the next thing without rewarding ourselves for what we've done. Think of this as positive reinforcement!

Talk about how you're doing

Once you're into the swing of this, I want you to start sharing the successes you're proud of and to talk more about your life and work. This is another area that can be difficult – self-deprecation is considered polite and you can feel boastful talking about yourself, or you might worry that others will react negatively towards you or that being confident makes you unlikeable.

I'm not asking you to shout about your successes from the rooftops or to tell everyone you know about them, just to discuss them with the people you care about. This will give you a chance to connect to them better. Modesty does not mean denying your success and talking about something doesn't mean bragging about it; simply think about what you feel comfortable sharing with the people you care about.

There's a wider lesson from this too; it's not right to feel bad about doing well or to feel that we need to play ourselves down to be more acceptable! Having confidence is a good thing, talking about the things you are proud of and that are going well is something we should all be doing. It's only by doing this that we can become more comfortable with our success and it will feel more acceptable.

Embrace acceptance

Before reading this book you probably felt uncertain about who you would be without your imposter identity, but I hope you can now see that this is not who you are: you are so much more than this. To become truly comfortable in your skin you need to be aware of and comfortable with showing *all* of yourself – the parts you like and the parts you're not so sure about.

When we stop judging ourselves and hiding the parts of ourselves that we imagine others wouldn't like we can secure a more positive sense of who we are. We then have a chance to see that others will accept not just the polished version that gets everything right, but the messy parts too. Acknowledging this frees you to be yourself confidently and this self-acceptance and connection to others is key to living a happy and healthy life.

Acceptance also means trusting in life, letting go of control and recognizing that you can't be responsible for how everything goes. Life doesn't always run smoothly, no matter how hard you try to make it and in aiming to prevent anything ever going wrong you have been causing yourself much greater stress. Instead allow life to happen; it will carry on just fine without you trying to keep tight control over it. You cannot guarantee that it will always run smoothly, but it will be much more enjoyable when you approach it in this way.

Step out of your comfort zone

Thanks to imposter syndrome you may have become quite comfortable with putting things off in some areas, avoiding them or not trying as hard as you could. For too long what you know has felt comfortable, even though it hasn't been working that well. This has meant that you haven't risked taking on new challenges or chasing what you really want. You might have believed that hiding away and not challenging yourself would make life easier, but it means living with feelings of insecurity, guilt and regret.

And what exactly are you gaining by avoiding any risks? It may be a safe life, but is it a happy and fulfilled one?

The final step is to embrace the discomfort you've been avoiding for so long. Understanding the limits of your comfort zone and taking steps to venture outside it is hugely important for you from now on. New experiences, new hobbies and challenging yourself on a regular basis are massively important for maintaining good mental health, personal growth and improving self-esteem. It's only when you venture outside familiar territory that you really discover what you're made of.

When you start to challenge yourself, push your personal boundaries and step into a new zone, this pushes you into a space where stress levels are slightly higher than normal. You step out of your comfort zone and become fully focused on what you're doing. With this comes a natural momentum together with ambition and a drive to learn new things. The more you do this, the easier you'll find it as you become accustomed to this state of productive discomfort. This will give you a chance to reach your potential and discover what you're capable of.

You need to become comfortably uncomfortable if you want to overcome imposter syndrome. The little voice in your head will still try to come up with reasons to throw you off course, but listen to the new voice you have built through reading this book. This is the voice to trust. You need to face things you've been shying away from so you can prove to yourself that you can cope and you are good enough. Yes, you'll feel afraid, but soon you'll become used to this and you'll notice the benefits, which are so worthwhile.

To get started, set yourself some goals:

- Think about your hopes and aspirations, new things you want to do or try out, places you'd like to visit

- What challenges could you set yourself that you've been putting off or avoiding?
- Think about the ways your feelings have hindered your career progression and then take deliberate countermeasures, such as going for promotions and looking out for exciting job opportunities
- When your mind says 'don't', do the opposite. Don't go for the promotion? Going for it is exactly what you need to do. Don't speak up? Voice your thoughts and let others respond to them

Pick a few goals to try out. When you step out of your comfort zone be willing to feel uncomfortable and move through your fear.

Remind yourself:

- Everyone feels discomfort in new situations
- It's normal to feel out of your depth when you try something new
- It's better to try than to never know
- You need to learn to enjoy the thrill
- Reframing discomfort will show you its benefits

As I said at the beginning of the chapter, being comfortable with yourself and confident in your abilities is the ultimate protection against imposter syndrome, so try to work on these aspects of your character regularly. Think of the effort you put into convincing yourself you were an imposter and how far you could go if you put the same effort into this.

Conclusion: Moving forward with confidence

Your work here has only just started. Together we've planted the seeds of change; it's now up to you to look after them, to water and nurture them, so they continue to flower year after year. The imposter part is the vulnerable part of you and like a flower it needs compassion and care. The more you build on these new ways of thinking and incorporate healthy coping strategies into your daily life, the easier it will be to hold on to this new view, so you continue to flourish and build trust in yourself.

I hope you have been able to question the views you held about yourself and think about what you want from your life from now on. You should be feeling very different from when you started and be able to see that you are *not* an imposter. The way you were living your life was keeping you trapped rather than safe.

By daring to go against the imposter voice you will have seen that you *are* capable, you deserve success and you can believe in yourself. This new view of yourself will bring an inner calm and self-assurance to whatever you do. You now have the freedom to live your life as you want to. You are enough, right now, exactly as you are.

What does success mean to you?

I've left this question until the end, as I didn't want the imposter voice to have any say in what success means to you. Before this book, success was your antidote to feeling like an imposter. It should now be abundantly clear that your old approach to life just didn't work. It gave you no joy or satisfaction, no reward for doing well. When you become obsessed by that final goal – thinking, hoping and scheming about what's ahead – it can blind you to the adventure of life and its real purpose: living.

Now you understand the flaws in this approach and the mind-trap of imposter syndrome, is it worth sacrificing everything for that version of success? I'm not sure what your answer will be, but I do know that to live a healthy and happy life and to wave goodbye to the imposter for good you need to think about yourself and your needs. You've been so busy keeping the mask on that you've forgotten what you want.

Now you can see that you don't have to push your life forward and control everything – it is much more enjoyable to let life happen. It's time to give yourself permission to invest in yourself and live life your way.

Standing at your new vantage point, I want you to take a step back and give yourself some time to think about what success means to you now. It's this that will shape how you choose to move forward, offering a road map and checks that you're on the right course.

Take some time to think about what you really want from your life. Not what you think you should do, or what others expect you to do. What do *you* want? Listen to the compassionate voice that knows what's best for you and what you need from life.

Ask yourself:

- What does success mean to me now?
- What do I want for myself?
- What do I want from my life?
- What do I want from my relationships?
- What's it all for?

In my mind, success is not just about one thing. It's a layered experience that reflects how you integrate all the different elements of your life – your family, friends, hobbies, interests, passions. Real success comes when you manage to include everything that is important to you. Once you have answered these questions, write down your personal recipe for success in your notebook or wherever you have been keeping notes. Call it 'My Personal Recipe for Success'.

Success is different for everyone, but by working out what it means to you you are giving yourself a reason for seeking it. This can act as a check going forward, keeping you on track.

The imposter voice may still lurk in the background, telling you all the reasons this new way won't work – that you'd be mad to lower your standards, that you'll miss the satisfaction of doing things perfectly and that you won't get where you need to be. If you get caught in the imposter trap look back at your personal recipe for success and question which approach is best for getting what you really want from life.

Review your progress

Now take some time to review everything you have done. This is something I do in therapy to help consolidate all your ideas while they are fresh in your mind. It gives you something to look at when you need it, so you have an easy reminder without having to go back through everything in this book. Take your time doing this and note it down in your notebook or somewhere you can easily refer to it.

First look back to the commitment you made at the start. What were the three most important changes you hoped to make? Have you managed them? I hope you *have* achieved your goals and gained what you wanted from this book. Ask yourself what you need to do to keep going with these ideas. Is there anything you still need to work on?

Next, I want you to look back at everything you have written down as you worked through this book and completed each of the strategies.

- When you read the book, which ideas resonated most with you?
- What was most helpful in terms of understanding imposter syndrome and how it operates?
- Which chapters really struck a chord?
- Which skills and strategies did you find particularly helpful?
- Which are the key ideas you want to pursue?
- How can you do this?
- Who can support you?

Make a note of the ideas you want to take forward and put some reminders in your diary to check how you're doing over the coming months. This will help you to keep them in mind and keep working at them. Consider telling family and friends what you're doing, if you haven't already. Their encouragement will be invaluable.

Some days it will seem easy and other days it will feel hard. The difficult days are when you will need to remember the new ideas most; the more you use them the easier it will become as you build those new pathways. It is worth persevering, I promise. When you need to, make sure you look back at your notes, remind yourself of this review and be kind to yourself so you can get back on track.

Be careful about what you expect of yourself and continue to monitor this. Remember that no one feels great every day and it's normal to feel nervous at times. Do not conclude from this information that you are not up to the task; it simply means you're human.

Recognize your warning bells

Next, think about your warning bells. How you think about imposter syndrome has fundamentally changed, but the old fears may still pop up now and again and it can be all too easy to slip back into old habits. To avoid this, think about how imposter syndrome used to operate in your life. These are your warning signs. When you notice them recurring, it's a signal that the imposter is back.

Telltale signs might be:

- Overworking
- Perfectionism
- Fear of failure
- Avoidance
- Procrastination
- Self-criticism
- Self-doubt
- Insecurity

If it does come back, don't just wait for it to go again. Be proactive in tackling any problems, take a look at the notes from this review – and go back to the book if you need to. Stopping and re-evaluating might seem a luxury, but it's something we should all be doing regularly. If you just keep going and going, nothing can change.

Think of this as a top-up session. Reread your favourite parts and start using the strategies again. It's a bit like taking a painkiller for a headache; just because you've taken it once doesn't mean it won't work again the next time you have a headache. If you've found the ideas helpful, they will continue to be helpful in future. You know this new way works better for you; you just need a reminder.

If you are still struggling and this doesn't work, go and see your GP. They may suggest seeing a therapist who can help you put these ideas into practice and overcome any problems you're encountering.

Remember these key ideas

Finally, here are a few key ideas to take forward:

- You are not alone; almost everyone feels like an imposter at some point in their lives
- Remember what it means to be human
- Compassion, compassion, compassion
- Everyone experiences discomfort and it can be a good thing leading to personal growth
- Everyone experiences insecurity and self-doubt
- Perfection doesn't exist
- Failure is an important part of learning and building resilience
- We are made up of many parts
- It's impossible to stay on top of everything all the time
- Keep talking to others about imposter syndrome
- Life's an adventure not a race

Congratulations; you've reached the end of the book. You should feel very proud of yourself and all that you've done. Making these changes will have been – and will continue to be – hard. Recognizing how far you have come is really important. Don't underestimate what you have achieved.

Now all that's left for me to do is to wish you all the best. Keep going with all these new ideas and remember there's no magic formula; you need to find out what works best for *you*. Be kind to yourself and continue to work on accepting and becoming more comfortable with who you are. When you know that you are enough, everything else changes and this knowledge will permeate everything you do.

Change is often filled with uncertainty. However, instead of concentrating on what could go wrong, take life a step at a time. My motto is, 'The small steps lead to the greatest changes.' Take each day as it comes and continually remind yourself of all the things that could go right, rather than wrong. It's also helpful to remember that change is an ongoing process and that you never stop growing and evolving.

Take one last moment to look at all you've done. I hope you can see just how strong you are. Hold on to this and find somewhere to put it securely inside yourself. And remember that imposter syndrome is not something that makes you different. Let's stop keeping it a secret and instead talk openly about how it operates, so it can no longer claw its way into our lives.

Endnote

I've learned that clinical psychologists tend to be drawn to topics that resonate personally. Often we don't realize why they have a pull on us until much later. It turns out that this book is about one of those topics. It is one I thought I knew a lot about, but in fact I was like the friend who thought he was brilliant at French. I didn't realize how vast the subject was, how all the problems connected or how it might apply to me. It also turns out that writing a book on your own is *much* harder than I expected!

When I started writing this book I didn't think imposter syndrome was something that affected me much. Yes, definitely when it came to standing up and speaking at events and when it came to writing this book, but in my day-to-day work I've always felt fairly confident. Yet, as I've written this book, I've realized that I fall into many imposter traps.

I spend very little time thinking about my successes and I have always put my achievements down to the fact that I have worked really hard – something anyone can do. I frequently move the goalposts and move on to the next challenge before taking on board the success of the last – and I'm so busy that even if I wanted to stop and think about everything I wouldn't have the time!

The Imposter Cure has taught me some important lessons to take forward and has made me reassess how I've got to where I am now. It's a relief to see that I'm doing well, not thanks to fluke, but through a combination of hard work, a love of psychology and determination. This has really helped me start to internalize my achievements and see that luck and contacts are only a small part of the story.

As I struggled with writing the book I could remind myself that I was finding it hard because writing a book *is* hard, bringing a more realistic and kinder approach to tackling each chapter. This helped me to keep going when I felt like giving up!

When it came to writing about perfectionism, I had no concern that this would relate to me. I knew I wasn't a perfectionist as I don't do anything perfectly, so it couldn't apply. But I soon realized how wrong I was. I recognized the personal descent from working hard on one project to working hard on every project. I recognized the way perfectionism narrows your life, the push to keep doing more and – most of all – the idea that you can exhaust yourself in an attempt to do 'enough'.

This made me think: if what you do is never enough, why not pick the bits you like best and do a bit less, something I'm now trying to put into practice. That's the great thing about re-evaluating. It helps you see everything more clearly and make choices, rather than carrying on without ever looking up and seeing that what you're doing might not be working any more.

Writing this book has come at a reflective time in my life as my middle child has just started going to school and I'm at home for the first time with just my youngest. I can see the passage of time and I keep asking myself: how do I want to look back on things? This is an easy question for me to answer; I want to look back and remember the time I spent with my family, the most important thing in my life, and my friends. I want to be proud of my career *and* to have enjoyed my work.

It seems simple, yet things can easily get in the way. You have to go against what's expected and do what's right for you. Most of all, you have to go against the part of you that asks whether anyone really gets to do this, as if it's a luxury you're not entitled to. What I saw through writing this book is that the person asking those questions is the imposter and that if you want to live the life that is right for you, that voice does not give you the answers. If you're ready to change and you want to, then you make the changes. You *can* find a way to do this; the only thing stopping you is you.

The night before writing this endnote, I watched the London African Gospel Choir performing *Graceland* and, oddly, it brought everything together for me. This is the album I've listened to most in my life. First in the car with my parents and my siblings, then as an adult with my husband, then in the car with one child, then two, then three. As they sang 'These are the days of miracle and wonder' it made me think. *These are the days*. Life is filled with so much potential, but also so many challenges. We might not have much choice about the challenges, but we do have a choice about how we spend our days.

I really hope this book has done the same for you and that you now have a new way of looking at yourself and can see all you are capable of. Believe in yourself!

Notes

Notes

Notes

References, resources and further reading

Chapter 1

29 **'Imposter syndrome was first described':** Clance, P. R. & Imes, S. (1978), 'The imposter phenomenon in high achieving women: Dynamics and therapeutic intervention', *Psychotherapy: Theory, Research & Practice*, 15, 241–7

34 **'just how harmful imposter syndrome can be':** Neureiter, M. & Traut-Mattausch, E. (2016), 'Inspecting the Dangers of Feeling like a Fake: An Empirical Investigation of the Imposter Phenomenon in the World of Work', *Frontiers in Psychology*, 7:1445

40 **'discovered that imposters experience failure-related shame':** Young, V. (2011) *The Secret Thoughts of Successful Women: Why Capable People Suffer from the Imposter Syndrome and How to Thrive in Spite of it*, New York: Crown Business

Chapter 3

61 **'if you are naturally more prone to worrying and anxiety':** Casselman, S. E. (1991), 'The imposter phenomenon in medical students: Personality correlates and developmental issues' (Doctoral dissertation, Virginia Consortium for Professional Psychology), *Dissertations Abstracts International*, 53, 5-B

Chae, J. H., Piedmont, R. L., Estadt, B. K. & Wicks, R. J. (1995), 'Personological evaluation of Clance's Imposter Phenomenon Scale in a Korean sample', *Journal of Personality Assessment*, 65(3), 468–85

Chapter 4

78 **'Confirmation bias':** Festinger, L. (1957), *A Theory of Cognitive Dissonance*, Stanford: Stanford University Press

Chapter 5

100 **'She collected her observations':** Ware, B. (2012), *The Top Five Regrets of the Dying: A Life Transformed by the Dearly Departing*, London: Hay House

102 **'avoidant coping strategies are a psychological risk':** Holahan, C. J. & Moos, R. H. (1987), 'Risk, resistance, and psychological distress: A longitudinal analysis with adults and children', *Journal of Abnormal Psychology*, 96(1), 3–13

Taylor, S. in collaboration with the Psychosocial Working Group (1998), 'Coping Strategies', https://macses.ucsf.edu/research/psychosocial/coping.php (accessed 13 February 2019)

Chapter 7

123 **'self-criticism makes you *less* effective at implementing coping strategies':** Powers, T. A., Koestner, R. & Zuroff, D. C. (2007), 'Self-criticism, goal motivation, and goal progress', *Journal of Social and Clinical Psychology*, vol. 26, no. 7

McGonigal, K. (2011), *The Willpower Instinct: How Self-Control Works, Why It Matters, and What You Can Do to Get More of It*, New York: Avery

132 **'defined self-compassion as being made up of three main components':** Neff, K. D. (2003), 'Self-compassion: An alternative conceptualization of a healthy attitude toward oneself', *Self and Identity*, 2, 85–102

133 **'Self-compassion ... leads to greater happiness':** Leary, M. R., Tate, E. B., Adams, C. E., Batts Allen, A. & Hancock, J. (2007), 'Self-compassion and reactions to unpleasant self-relevant events: The implications of treating oneself kindly', *Journal of Personality and Social Psychology*, 92(5), 887–904

Neff, K. D., Rude, S. S. & Kirkpatrick, K. L. (2007), 'An examination of self-compassion in relation to positive psychological functioning and personality traits', *Journal of Research in Personality*, 41, 908–916

Chapter 8

143 **'social isolation is associated with heightened risk of disease and early death':** Cacioppo et al (2002), 'Loneliness and Health: Potential Mechanisms', *Psychosomatic Medicine*, 64, 407–17

143 **'warm and supportive relationships have long-term benefits for health and longevity':** Taylor, S. E. & Gonzaga, G. C., 'Evolution, Relationships, and Health: The Social Shaping Hypothesis' in Schaller, M., Simpson, J. A. & Kenrick, D. T. (2006), *Evolution and Social Psychology (Frontiers of Social Psychology)*, 1st edition, New York and Hove: Psychology Press, pp. 211–236

Chapter 9

160 **'They don't make you happy either':** Kasser, T. & Ahuvia, A. (2002), 'Materialistic values and well-being in business students', *European Journal of Social Psychology*, 32(1), 137–146

Kasser, T. (2003), *The High Price of Materialism*, London: MIT Press

161 **'perfectionist tendencies are on the rise':** Curann, T. & Hill. A. P. (2017), 'Perfectionism is increasing over time: A meta-analysis of birth cohort differences from 1989 to 2016', *Psychological Bulletin*, 1–21

164 **'the higher the level of perfectionism':** Curann, T. & Hill. A. P. (2017), 'Perfectionism is increasing over time: A meta-analysis of birth cohort differences from 1989 to 2016', *Psychological Bulletin*, 1–21

Chapter 10

170 **'The research backs this up':** Thompson, T., Foreman, P., & Martin, F. (2000), 'Imposter fears and perfectionistic concern over mistakes', *Personality and Individual Differences*, 29(4), 629–47

170 **'Just as common illnesses build up your immune system':** Linley, P. A. & Joseph, S. (2004), 'Positive Change Following Trauma and Adversity: a review', *Journal of Traumatic Stress*, 17(1), 11–21

174 **'"Once you embrace unpleasant news"':** Gates, B. & Hemingway, C. (2000), *Business @ the Speed of Thought: Succeeding in the Digital Economy*, New York: Warner Books, p184

178 **'we regret what we don't do much more than what we do':** Gilovich, T. & Medvec, V. H. (1994), 'The temporal pattern to the experience of regret', *Journal of Personality and Social Psychology*, 67(3), 357–65

Chapter 11

189 **'Gladwell calls it the 10,000 hour rule':** Gladwell, M. (2008), *Outliers: The Story of Success*, New York: Little, Brown

190 **'timing was the top reason for success':** Gross, B. (2015), 'The single biggest reason why start-ups succeed', https://www.ted.com/talks/bill_gross_the_single_biggest_reason_why_startups_succeed?language=en (accessed 20 February 2019)

194 **'85 per cent of all jobs are filled thanks to networking':** Adler, L. (2016) 'New Survey reveals 85% of All Jobs are Filled via Networking' https://www.linkedin.com/pulse/new-survey-reveals-85-all-jobs-filled-via-networking-lou-adler/?trk=hp-feed-article-title-like&trk=v-feed (accessed 29th March 2019)

Chapter 12

204 **'journalist Oliver Burkeman's TEDx talk':**
Burkeman, O. (2011), 'How to Stop Fighting
Against Time', https://www.youtube.com/
watch?v=XtfCmhPr-J8 (accessed 28 March 2019)

208 **'one of the most effective things you can
do is forgive yourself for procrastinating':**
Wohl, M., Pychyl, T. & Bennett, S. (2010), 'I forgive
myself, now I can study: How self-forgiveness for
procrastinating can reduce future procrastination',
Personality and Individual Differences, 48(7), 803–8

212 **'people who are grateful are happier':** Emmons,
R. A. & McCullough, M. E. (2003), 'Counting Blessings
Versus Burdens: An Experimental Investigation of
Gratitude and Subjective Well-Being in Daily Life',
Journal of Personality and Social Psychology, 84(2), 377–89

Emmons, R. A. (2007), *Thanks! How the New
Science of Gratitude Can Make You Happier*,
Boston: Houghton Mifflin Harcourt

Chapter 13

216 **'found that participants scoring in the bottom
quartile':** Kruger, J. & Dunning, D. (1999), 'Unskilled
and unaware of it: how difficulties in recognizing one's
own incompetence lead to inflated self-assessments',
Journal of Personality and Social Psychology, 77(6), 1121–34

Chapter 14

229 **'as much as 40 per cent is linked to our
intentional daily activities':** Lyubomirsky, S.,
Sheldon, K. M. & Schkade, D. (2005), 'Pursuing
Happiness: The Architecture of Sustainable
Change', *Review of General Psychology*, 9(2), 111–31

231 **'One study asked people to write down their worries':** Leahy, R. L. (2005), *The Worry Cure: Seven Steps to Stop Worry from Stopping You*, New York: Harmony Books

Chapter 15

251 **'A study published in the *European Journal of Social Psychology*':** Briñol, P., Petty, R. E. & Wagner, B. (2009), 'Body posture effects on self-evaluation: A self-validation approach', *European Journal of Social Psychology*, 39(6), 1053–64

251 **'Power posing has also hit the headlines':** Cuddy, A. (2015), *Presence: Bringing Your Boldest Self to Your Biggest Challenges*, New York: Little, Brown

Cuddy, A., 'Your body language may shape who you are' (2012), www.ted.com/talks/amy_cuddy_your_body_language_shapes_who_you_are?language=en (accessed 20 February 2019)

Resources and further reading

- Dudău, D. P. (2014), 'The Relation between Perfectionism and Imposter Phenomenon', *Procedia – Social and Behavioral Sciences*, 127, 129–33
- Hutchins, H. M. & Rainbolt, H. (2017), 'What triggers imposter phenomenon among academic faculty? A critical incident survey exploring antecedents, coping, and development opportunities', *Human Resource Development International*, 20(3), 194–214
- Sakulku, J. & Alexander, J. (2011), 'The Imposter Phenomenon', *International Journal of Behavioural Science*, 6(1), 73–92
- VIA Survey of Character Strengths: www.viacharacter.org

Index

Acknowledgements

Jack, Max, Edie and Bibi – the loves of my life – everything is better with you. The ultimate gang, I'm so happy we're on this adventure together. You brighten my days and in the difficult times remind me why it's all worthwhile.

To my in-house copy editor/husband Jack, thank you for supporting me to write this book, for your brilliant ideas and tireless patience, for reading and re-reading, for reassuring me and, most of all, for always believing in me and for loving me no matter what.

My wonderful parents, John and Deborah, whose quiet, unwavering stability has kept me grounded. It took me having children to really appreciate all you do, but I now realize how lucky I am to know you're always on the end of the phone and that I have a second home to go to.

My brilliant sister Susannah, who put up with all my questions and who is not just a great sister, but also a great friend. Alice, who kept everything and everyone going (including me!) while I was at work. My brother Michael for reminding me of the Dunning-Kruger effect. And my friends and extended family for always being there.

My wonderful agent Jane, for your support of me over the years – even when the ideas and writing I sent you were a long way from ever being book material! I'd have given up on me a long time ago. It's your straight-talking advice and encouragement that has slowly inched me towards writing this book.

My fantastic editor Kate, who took a chance on me and whose amazing ideas, enthusiasm and knowledge are infectious. Thanks also to the brilliant team at Octopus, particularly Ella for her detailed, considered and incredibly thoughtful edit of this book.

Thank you to the psychologists and health professionals who I've worked with and learned from. I feel very fortunate to work in such an exciting field that is constantly evolving and filled with so many people with brilliant ideas.

And finally, thank you to the amazing people I work with in my clinic. Your strength and courage always humble me and I feel privileged to be let into your lives. If this book is inspired by anybody, it is you.

About the author

Dr Jessamy Hibberd (BSc, MSc, DClinPsy, PgDip) is a highly respected chartered clinical psychologist, author and commentator. She has 14 years' experience working in mental health (within both the NHS and in her own practice) and is passionate about psychology and the benefits it can bring.

Jessamy works one-to-one with adults experiencing common mental health problems such as depression, anxiety or low self-esteem. Her experience with this client group makes her the perfect professional to write a book on imposter syndrome.